The Partisan War:
The South Carolina
Campaign of 1780-1782

RUSSELL F. WEIGLEY is professor of history at Temple
University in Philadelphia, Pennsylvania.

The Partisan War:
The South Carolina
Campaign of 1780-1782

Russell F. Weigley

TRICENTENNIAL BOOKLET NUMBER 2

Published for the South Carolina Tricentennial Commission
by the University of South Carolina Press
Columbia, South Carolina

International Standard Book Number: 0-87249-133-1

Library of Congress Catalog Card Number: 78-113804

Manufactured in the United States of America
By Vogue Press, Inc.

Contents

Introduction

"You see that we must again resume the partisan war."

—Nathanael Greene

The travail of American forces in Vietnam has made unconventional war a subject of fascinated interest in the United States. The dedication of many Communists to irregular "wars of national liberation" as a means of advancing their cause is all too likely to maintain the interest of the subject.

The twentieth-century United States has not adjusted easily to involvement in irregular war. Our immense wealth and productivity, our great resources of manpower, and our national conviction that war is an abnormal condition, completely distinct from peace, and a condition which should be terminated quickly and in a complete, clear-cut decision, all equipped us admirably to fight and win the two world wars. But they do not fit us so well for limited wars in climate and terrain where massive military power can be in some ways a liability, where victory itself is almost undefinable, and where enemies fight elusively and with methods so thoroughly opposed to conventional rules of war that many of the textbook principles for its conduct are stood on their heads and bring only boomerang results.

On the other hand, the difficulties visited on us by Communist employment of irregular war have sometimes led to exaggerated impressions of the newness of this sort of war. General Vo Nguyen Giap, the North Vietnamese

1

hero of Dienbienphu and thorn in the American side, did
not invent irregular war. Nor did Mao Tse-tung, although
Mao especially is a brilliant theoretician of such war, and
both are formidable enemies partly because of their acute
perceptions of the nature of irregular war. The United
States in recent years has had to wrench itself from accustomed military habits to cope with irregular war, but
our own earlier past was not without experience of it, in
many of the Indian campaigns, especially those against the
Seminoles in Florida, and perhaps most notably in the South
Carolina campaign of 1780–1782 during the American Revolution. In the latter campaign Americans themselves became improvisers of irregular war, and in one of the first
guerrilla campaigns of modern history they played skill-
fully against the British a role paralleling that of the Spanish guerrillas against Napoleon, T. E. Lawrence's Arabs
against the Turks, and Giap's Viet Minh against the French.

The purpose of this narrative is to view the South
Carolina campaign of the later years of the Revolution
through the perspective of our recent insights into unconventional war. Communist theories of the war of national
liberation may no longer seem so mysteriously formidable
when they are illustrated by the actions of Francis Marion
and Nathanael Greene. Nevertheless, it remains true that
the South Carolina campaign of 1780–1782 was one in which
the role of the Americans was analogous to that of the Viet
Minh or the Viet Cong, and with similar resources the
American rebels emerged triumphant; while it was the
British whose part was analogous to that of the French or
Americans in Vietnam, and they ended in defeat. Guerrilla
uprisings actively supported by even a small proportion of
the population in the theater of war are extremely hard
to subdue, and while the South Carolina experience may
erase some of the aura of exoticism and mystery which sur-

rounds Communist irregular war, it offers anything but comfort about the tangible problems of coping with it.

Though we must be prepared to struggle in whatever way necessary to protect our own security, to some degree this note of pessimism may be just as well. Our current fascination with unconventinal war, even though Communist use of it frightens us and the Vietnam experience appalls us, has invested irregular war with a kind of glamorous appeal, embodied for example in President John F. Kennedy's exaltation of the United States Army Special Forces, the Green Berets. We should be distrustful of any tendency to glamorize irregular war. Irregular war is not only utterly unglamorous in reality but extremely hard to win. In addition, because it puts a premium upon breaking rules and doing anything to win (while conventional war does at least adhere to certain rules and customs), because almost the essence of irregular war is that anything goes, irregular war can well plant an infection of lawlessness and brutalization in any society that becomes involved in it. By helping to invest irregular war with glamor, John Kennedy helped invest rule-breaking violence with glamor; the irony of what followed is too obvious to require comment.

This narrative focuses upon events in South Carolina, but the race to the Dan and the Guilford Court House campaign of 1781 so much determined everything that followed within South Carolina, that it has been necessary to include those campaigns waged in the sister state to the north and spilling over into Virginia.

The Partisan War

Charleston and the Waxhaws: 1779–May 29, 1780

"The Americans would be less dangerous if they had a regular army."

—Major General Frederick Haldimand

Writing of Spain's desperate struggle against Napoleon in the early nineteenth century, the British military critic Sir Basil Henry Liddell Hart has emphasized the paradox that it was to Spain's great good fortune that her regular army was defeated. "The French had beaten," he says, "and continued to beat, any regular Spanish forces, but the thoroughness of these defeats was of the greatest benefit to the defeated. For it ensured that the main effort of the Spanish was thrown into guerrilla warfare. An intangible web of guerrilla bands replaced a vulnerable military target. . . ."

The same words could apply equally well to South Carolina's struggle for independence after the British army reconquered the state in 1780. Throughout the War of American Independence, the armed forces of the Revolution, with the exception of a few unusually well officered regiments and companies, never could stand up to the British army in pitched battle in the open field. The weapons technology of eighteenth-century warfare demanded rigorous discipline and prolonged training to permit the battlefield maneuvering of large numbers of men in rigid lines. The smoothbore muskets of the day had a maximum

4

effective range of eighty to one hundred yards and, without rear sights, a practical range which was far less. They were effective weapons only for disciplined volley firing. Artillery heavy enough to inflict much damage on the enemy was generally too heavy and unwieldy to be maneuvered on the battlefield. Because of these limitations in weaponry, battles were won by disciplined, unbreaking lines of men falling upon the enemy with the bayonet. The newly formed armies of Revolutionary America, with few trained and experienced officers and proportionately far fewer trained and experienced sergeants to drill the rank and file, could not match the British army in the disciplined application of volley firing and the climactic bayonet charge which won eighteenth-century battles.

Therefore efforts to raise and train armies which might challenge the British to pitched battle were often misdirected efforts which led to waste and unnecessary sacrifice. George Washington, a soldier of a conservative cast of mind who had gained much of his military experience while serving with British regulars in the French and Indian War, tried to mold the Continental Army of the Revolution into as close as possible an approximation of the British regular army. His efforts were not altogether in vain, because his approximation of a regular army served as a permanent core of resistance to the British which was probably indispensable to keeping the Revolution alive. But experience led Washington to become less and less willing—after Brandywine, almost totally unwilling—to risk his army in conflict with the whole of the main British army in America under circumstances of equal tactical advantage; he had to fight a war of raids on outposts and detachments, of rear-guard actions, of sieges, and in general of attrition. Less cautious commanders than Washington were likely to be misled into error when they had at hand troops who in

theory were regulars, but who in fact could not compete in
conventional war against the veteran soldiers of King George
III.

In this manner Major General Benjamin Lincoln was
misled, in the events which opened the way to British
reconquest of South Carolina, with the result that he use-
lessly sacrificed his army. At the end of 1779 Major General Sir Henry Clinton of the British army decided to make
a second attempt to capture the city of Charleston (his first
attempt, centering upon the famous bombardment of William Moultrie's fort in 1776, had failed because Sir Peter
Parker's mismanagement of the Royal Navy's part in the
assault prevented the army from coming to grips with the
defenders). Lincoln, the American commander in the
South, decided to make a formal defense of the city. He
was encouraged to do so by the presence in his command
of the whole South Carolina contingent of the Continental
Line—the Revolutionary approximation of a regular army—
plus a promised reinforcement of large portions of the
Continental regiments of North Carolina and Virginia.

Although Lincoln's reinforcement arrived, Clinton led
against him a British force of 10,000 soldiers, supported by
a large fleet with 5,000 seamen. Lincoln's defenders, about
2,650 Continentals and 2,500 South Carolina militia—short-
term state troops called to arms for the emergency—were
neither skillful nor numerous enough to avoid being bottled
up in Charleston by naval blockade on the one side and
Clinton's army, controlling the Neck between the Ashley
and Cooper rivers, on the other. For a short time while
Clinton prepared to besiege him, Lincoln might have led
his army through a narrow escape route up the Cooper
River to Monck's Corner, where Brigadier General Isaac
Huger of South Carolina stood with about 500 men, including more South Carolina militia and some Continental

cavalry. But his own indecisive temperament and the pleas of Lieutenant Governor Christopher Gadsden and the Charleston citizenry not to abandon the town caused Lincoln to ponder that plan until it was too late.

A young British cavalryman with a good record in the northern campaigns, Lieutenant Colonel Banastre Tarleton, led his Legion—a word denoting a mixed cavalry and infantry command—against Monck's Corner. Major Patrick Ferguson supported him with his organization of Loyalist marksmen. Tarleton and Ferguson struck Huger's force at three o'clock in the morning of April 14, 1780, routed it, and with the aid of infantry reinforcements closed the escape route. Monck's Corner marked the beginning of Tarleton's reputation as a major figure of the war. The alleged hacking to death of a rebel major who had surrendered also marked the beginning of Tarleton's reputation as a butcher.

On May 12, Lincoln surrendered Charleston and his army. All his Continental soldiers became prisoners of war, and all his militia became prisoners on parole. Together they represented almost the whole organized military strength of the Revolution in South Carolina. Practically all of the little that remained, 350 Virginia Continentals and a small party of Lieutenant Colonel William Washington's Continental cavalry, together under the command of Colonel Abraham Buford, were beaten and dispersed by Tarleton with his Legion of Loyalists and forty British regulars of the 17th Dragoons at the Waxhaws settlement near the North Carolina border on May 29. The cutting down of rebels who asked for quarter on this occasion began to make the phrase "Tarleton's quarter" a byword for cruelty; Tarleton said his men could not be restrained because they had seen his horse shot from under him and thought he had been killed.

British and Loyalist detachments now ranged throughout South Carolina, receiving the submission of the state's
rebel militia officers and placing all former rebels on
parole. The American War apparently had turned a corner
towards British victory. For two years previously, save for
successes in remote and thinly populated Georgia, the
British had faced frustrating stalemate. Now, in contrast,
the pivotal state of the whole South lay at their feet, North
Carolina seemed open before them, and beyond the Carolinas even Virginia might be ripe for conquest.

Perhaps all might have remained so if the King's officers
in South Carolina had been better statesmen than they
proved to be. Nevertheless, even on the morrow of the fall
of Charleston the British situation was not nearly so good
nor the Revolutionary cause in the South nearly so ruined
as they seemed. There was much about the British position
in Charleston that resembled, to cite a recent analogy, the
situation of the French who returned to Hanoi to restore
colonial rule in Indochina in 1945. Like the French in Indochina, the British in South Carolina could count upon
considerable sympathy and assistance from many of the
inhabitants, from conservative men who favored the stability of the old regime and others who simply feared the
rebels more than they feared more familiar authority. But
opposed to Britain there remained a tough core of resistance,
which adversity seemed merely to stimulate, and which the
indomitable and ubiquitous rebel governor, John Rutledge,
tirelessly nourished. With conventional American military
power extinguished, furthermore, the resistance was willing
to embark upon new and irregular modes of war, destined
to prove far more deadly.

In 1780 the word "guerrilla" had not yet entered the
language. Desperate peoples had fought irregular wars since
the dawn of time, but recent European wars had become

so formalized and even ritualistic that the idea of irregular war had virtually passed beyond the ken of European armies. Even Indian wars in North America had made remarkably little impression upon the British army's formalized expectations about the nature of war. So the British army in South Carolina was badly prepared, in its strategic and tactical doctrine, in its systems of mobility, and in its psychology, for anything resembling guerrilla resistance.

The British army in South Carolina, furthermore, hung suspended at the end of a very long and very thin line of communications. By 1780 the War of American Independence had turned into a world war, with Great Britain pitted against France and Spain as well as the American rebels, while the Netherlands and the League of Armed Neutrals threatened to add to the company of her adversaries. The British navy had been allowed to decline since the Peace of Paris of 1763, and its strength no longer seemed adequate to guarantee the home islands against Franco-Spanish invasion while also guarding the empire in American waters, the Caribbean, the Mediterranean, and the Indian Ocean. The Admiralty gave first priority to defense of the invasion routes across the English Channel, and it so rationed ships that it conceded superior strength in North American waters to the French fleet for at least a short period annually. The army, too, was strained by the multiple demands of invasion defense and the empire; the driblet of reinforcements it felt able to spare for North America in 1779 and 1780 were so few that they were hardly worthy of the name.

The British army had come to South Carolina in these straitened circumstances largely because southern Loyalists offered assurance that a large Loyalist strength in the South in general and in South Carolina in particular awaited only British encouragement and protection to assert itself and

restore the area to the Crown. The rising of a great reservoir
of Loyalists was a will-o'-the-wisp which the British army
had pursued wherever it went in North America. Although
numerous Loyalists were indeed to be found in South Carolina, the Revolutionary government of the province had
gone so little challenged from 1775 until the coming of
Clinton's troops that anyone should have doubted the po-
tential of Loyalism to become a predominating force. The
British army came to South Carolina expecting to be sustained, despite the thinness of British resources and the
distance of transatlantic communication, by a rising of
South Carolina Loyalists. The South Carolina Loyalists, in
contrast, raised their heads upon Clinton's coming, expecting to be sustained by the British army and navy.

Thomas Sumter: May 29–July 25, 1780

"The pressure to meet terror with counterterror will at times seem
irresistible, but to do so is to play the guerrilla's game without his
particular advantages. Brutality, fear, and the resultant social dis-
organization can work only for the guerrillas, no matter who initiates
them."
—Peter Paret and John W. Shy, *Guerrillas in the 1960's*

Fanning out from Charleston to restore royal government everywhere in South Carolina, the British army estab-
lished garrisons at Georgetown and Beaufort as well as the
capital along the coast, and at Camden, Rocky Mount, and
Ninety-Six to shield the northern border of the province
and watch over the interior. Ninety-Six in the far west put
them in touch with the friendly, anti-Revolutionary Creek
and Cherokee Indians and threatened American settlements
beyond the mountains. In June, General Clinton felt secure

enough to return to his New York headquarters with about
one-third of the force that had taken Charleston, leaving
Major General Charles Lord Cornwallis with about 8,300
men to maintain and complete the conquest of the South.

Upcountry South Carolina was a frontier, and all frontier
districts in all the colonies harbored a large share of Loyalists, in part because frontiers especially felt the need of the
authority and protection of the Crown against the Indians,
in part because frontiersmen also hoped that British authority would offset the political weight of the coastal districts.
In South Carolina this latter consideration was unusually
important. By not creating counties and by malapportioning
the assembly, the lowcountry planters had kept the upcountry politically impotent. In the 1760's a Regulator
movement of disgruntled upcountrymen had fallen just short
of erupting in the sort of civil war that had torn North
Carolina. The upcountry tended to distrust anything the
lowcountry did; and because the lowland planters led the
Revolutionary movement, the upcountry tended to distrust
the Revolution as an event calculated simply to render them
still more subservient to the planters' political power. By
the time the war began, about half the population of South
Carolina resided in the upcountry, though with much less
than half the membership of the assembly.

Significantly, while the lowcountry supported the elimination of royal authority at the beginning of the Revolutionary War immediately and with little overt resistance,
it required warfare to assure the ascendancy of the Revolutionary cause in the upcountry. Armed bands of Loyalists
took the field in 1775 around Ninety-Six, and soon they
outnumbered a body of a thousand Revolutionary militia
which William Henry Drayton led against them under the
auspices of the Council of Safety in Charleston. Through
diplomacy Drayton managed to bring a kind of truce to the

area; but eventually some 1,800 of the Loyalists drove about 600 Revolutionaries under Major Andrew Williamson into the protection of the stockade at Ninety-Six. Colonels Richard Richardson and William Thompson then had to lead Revolutionary reinforcements from the low country and from North Carolina into the district; thus drawing upon men from outside the area, they were able to defeat one band of Loyalists in battle at Reedy River on November 22, 1775 and to overawe the others into disbanding. Just to the west, the Cherokee also opposed the Revolution; but fortunately they did not co-ordinate their actions with either the Loyalists or the British, and in 1776 Williamson led an expedition against them which considerably stunted their ability to make trouble.

Since that time, the frontier Loyalists of South Carolina had to bear harassment from their rebel neighbors supported by the Revolutionary government of the province and its armed militia. Upon the British capture of Charleston, the Loyalists predictably concluded that the time had come to repay their neighbors in kind. Clinton warned Cornwallis not to let anything happen that would entangle British troops in the interior, and Cornwallis wanted simply to maintain a safe quiet, which would free him for operations into North Carolina. On the other hand, the British set the Loyalists a bad example. Just before departing Clinton announced abandonment of the system whereby rebels were regarded as under parole and substituted a policy which offered full civil rights to all who showed complete loyalty, but punishment as enemies to any who did not; this compulsion of a clear choice between loyalty and a return to rebellion, when many would have preferred a neutrality which might have served Clinton just as well, perversely helped drive men back into rebellion. Presently Cornwallis proclaimed the confiscation of all property of forty-five leading Revolutionaries. Both generals permitted indiscriminate looting by their troops, including the seizures with which Tarleton remounted his cavalry upon South Carolina horses. The Scotch-Irish of the upcountry, hitherto largely indifferent to the war, were driven into the rebels' arms by a British policy of studied hostility to the Presbyterian church, based on the exaggerated assumption that religious dissent was synonymous with rebellion; Major James Wemyss, for example, burned the Presbyterian church at Indiantown, saying all Presbyterian churches were "sedition shops." Thus encouraged, Loyalists began a campaign of repayment of grievances by means of property seizures, house burnings, and personal harassment.

Such British obtuseness and Loyalist vengefulness provoked the result which Clinton had feared but did not have enough good sense to avoid, the coalescing of newly armed bands of rebels. In the clay hills of the Catawba River country, parties of armed Revolutionaries came together again under Colonels William Bratton and William Hill and Captains Edward Lacey, Jr., and John McClure. They attacked and bloodied groups of Loyalists in skirmishes near Winnsborough and Fishing Creek. These events in turn led Lieutenant Colonel George Turnbull of the New York (Loyalist) Volunteers, commanding Cornwallis's garrison at Rocky Mount, to send out some of his troops in further reprisal. Like many of the British occupation force, they were Loyalists from other provinces organized into quasi-regular units associated with the British army and trained and officered well enough that they resembled regular soldiers much more than did most of the American Continentals. A mixed cavalry and infantry force under Captain Christian Houk, or Huck, a Loyalist from Philadelphia, destroyed Colonel Hill's iron works and plundered the houses of Bratton and McClure. Captain Lacey's home

was inhabited by his Loyalist father and therefore escaped
Houk's attentions, whereupon the younger Lacey took his
father into custody to keep him from betraying information
to Houk. These unpleasant episodes, shaped by the bitter-
ness peculiar to fratricidal war, suggested the form the
conflict in South Carolina was henceforth increasingly to
take. Naturally, Captain Houk's reprisals angered enough
people to bring still further augmentation to the newly
restored rebel bands.

This first renewal of South Carolina resistance had no
plan or object save self-preservation and revenge, as is illustrated by the character and attitudes of the man who
became its principal military chieftain. Thomas Sumter
was a self-made, hard-bitten, and sometimes unscrupulous
farmer, miller, and magistrate, who lived in the Santee
River country above Eutaw Springs. He had served as lieutenant colonel of the Second Regiment of South Carolina
Riflemen at the successful defense of Charleston back in
1776, and as colonel of the Sixth South Carolina Continentals in Major General Robert Howe's Georgia campaign
in 1777 and 1778. In those campaigns he had shown neither
much distinction nor much sense of subordination to his
superior officers. In 1778, suffering from malaria and a
variety of other ailments, he resigned his commission. When
British columns advanced into the interior after the fall of
Charleston, however, Sumter thought it best, as a former
Revolutionary officer, to flee before them. His plantation
house happened to be in the path of Banastre Tarleton's
troops when that officer pursued Buford's remnant of Revolutionary resistance. Tarleton, who lacked the grievances
of the local Loyalists and whose only motives therefore
were cruelty and a misguided perception of the uses of
severity, let the Sumter place be burned down. In the Waxhaws and the territory called the New Acquisition, just

below the North Carolina border and west of the Catawba, an angry Sumter thereupon gathered round him similarly angry men to return to combat, not yet with any hope of redeeming South Carolina, but to fight for the sake of fighting.

A man of forty-six accustomed to being master of his own domain, Sumter had no more intention of subordinating himself to anyone else than before, and he soon elbowed rivals aside to win election by a special convention as brigadier general of South Carolina militia, thus becoming the ranking Revolutionary officer in the state. He had no particular sense of strategy either, but he did possess an overwhelming pugnaciousness reflected in the sobriquet which soon became familiar, the Carolina Gamecock. Characteristically, he decided to punish the enemy for Captain Houk's maraudings by attacking Rocky Mount itself. Repulsed there, he hit a strong Loyalist detachment at Hanging Rock, twelve miles away, where with about 800 men he broke into the enemy camp of about 500, killed or wounded some 200, but had to retreat because his men got drunk in the process of looting the enemy's supplies.

Sumter's and the other bands of armed rebels made no pretense of being able to face British or Loyalist regulars in formal battle. That was not their purpose. They rode almost everywhere they went and thus moved too fast for large British forces, especially infantry, to catch them. Although South Carolina was mostly wooded, west of the tidal marshes there was little underbrush, and this fact combined with hard sand and clay roads to make it one of the best areas for travel on horseback in America. In the forested upcountry hills, and especially around the Waxhaws, the rebel bands could scatter and find sanctuary after their attacks. When they struck the enemy, they relied on surprise and quick action. Although a few carried sabres for mounted combat, they did their fighting mostly on foot, sheltering themselves among the trees. Some carried rifles, which were too difficult to load and too susceptible to fouling for use by ordinary infantry, but which had immensely greater accuracy than smoothbore muskets and were therefore excellent for ambushes and hit-and-run raiding. Others made their smoothbore muskets more destructive by charging them with multiple pellets. Many were frontiersmen who could hit their targets reasonably well even with smoothbores.

Modern writers on irregular war, notably Mao Tse-tung and Vo Nguyen Giap, describe successful guerrilla campaigns as evolving from beginnings in simple terrorism, into planned campaigns featuring calculated strategy, and finally into full scale war when the guerrillas have so worn down the enemy that they can take the field openly against him. As General Giap puts it: ". . . it was necessary to accumulate thousands of small victories to turn them into a great success, thus gradually altering the balance of forces, in transforming our weakness into power. . . ." ". . . with the development of our forces, guerrilla warfare changed into a mobile warfare . . . our people's army constantly grew and passed from the stage of combats involving a section or company, to fairly large scale campaigns bringing into action several divisions."

In the spring of 1780, the rebel partisans in South Carolina were still in the stage of mounting terrorist attacks. Such harassing action compelled the British to disperse their forces over wider and wider areas and thus made them still more vulnerable. Nevertheless, despite the cumulative effects of terrorism in weakening the enemy's strength and will, terrorist campaigns alone are not likely to overcome an army as tough and well disciplined as was, whatever its deficiencies, Cornwallis's British army. Eventually the regular force would probably have broken and destroyed the guerrilla bands. To move on to the next phase of irregular war, the calculated strategic campaign, it is usually necessary, although not indispensable if the enemy is weak enough, to have the guerrillas supported by a nucleus of a regular army. A regular force, even if much weaker than the enemy's, can oblige the enemy to hold most of his army together in large units to deal with it; then the enemy cannot disperse enough to beat down the guerrillas. Fidel Castro's guerrillas managed to overthrow the weak Fulgencio Batista regime in Cuba without such support by a nucleus of regular soldiers; but the Duke of Wellington's British army in support of the Spanish guerrillas against Napoleon, Sir Edmund Allenby's army behind T. E. Lawrence's Arabs, and Giap's cadres of regulars along with the Viet Minh guerrillas were probably indispensable to those guerrillas' successes. So Sumter and the other South Carolina partisans also needed a restored Revolutionary army.

When Charleston fell, the admirable Major General Baron Jean de Kalb was marching southward with a small detachment of Continental troops from Washington's army. Washington, though no theorist or advocate of irregular war, thought de Kalb might serve some such function as just outlined in backing up the South Carolina irregulars until larger conventional forces could be restored to the South. De Kalb had little enough to serve as a nucleus of resistance, merely the Maryland and Delaware battalions of the Continental Line, 120 men who were the remnants of Count Casimir Pulaski's Legion, and eighteen guns of the First Continental Artillery Regiment. Nevertheless, while militia reinforcements from Virginia and North Carolina failed to join him as expected, de Kalb was highly resourceful and might well have made himself a rallying point for the parti-

sans. When the Continental Congress learned of Lincoln's
surrender, however, it resolved that a new commander less
foreign than de Kalb must go to the South, and it chose a
Congressional favorite, Major General Horatio Gates, late
of the British army, now of Virginia, and the victor of
Saratoga.

The avuncular and personally amiable "Granny" Gates
may deserve more of the credit for entrapping John Bur-
goyne's British army at Saratoga in 1777 than some historians have been willing to give him. But he was not the
general to retrieve the almost ruined southern situation.
He promptly showed he was not, by returning to conventional campaigning long before his force was adequate for it.

Camden, King's Mountain, and Francis Marion: July 25–December 2, 1780

"A people's war . . . should, like a kind of nebulous vapory essence,
nowhere condense into a solid body."

—Clausewitz

Gates and de Kalb were in agreement that their first
objective once they were strong enough to enter South
Carolina should be Camden on the Wateree River, taking
which would drive a wedge between the more westerly
British outposts and the enemy's bases on the coast. De
Kalb had planned a slow, strength-gathering, circuitous
march on Camden by way of Salisbury and Charlotte, North
Carolina. In these friendly settlements he hoped to pick
up recruits, and at the least he expected to keep the army
well fed. Gates, in contrast, once he assumed command on
July 25, proposed a direct advance straight to Camden from

the Deep River below Hillsborough. The trouble with this idea was that it would carry the army through sparsely populated pine barrens where there would be neither recruits nor food, and then into the Cross Creek region whose Scots Highland settlers, once Jacobite, had now transferred all the fervency of their loyalty to George III. It would also bring the army into contact with the enemy's main strength before time could allow either significant accretions to the American side or further depleting partisan strikes against the enemy.

For Gates it has to be said that he did arrange to bring about 1,200 North Carolina militia into his camps. But his march had the result which de Kalb feared, of bringing the army to Camden hungry and exhausted. Furthermore, Gates neglected to avail himself of the proffered help of William Washington and Lieutenant Colonel Anthony White with the survivors of Lincoln's cavalry, saying—despite the example of Tarleton—that cavalry was useless in the southern theater. Meanwhile Thomas Sumter made a characteristic contribution by proposing to raid the British line of communications between Camden and Charleston, if only Gates would reinforce him by detaching men and guns from the main army at the crisis of the campaign, just as Gates approached Camden with Cornwallis himself and the principal British force awaiting him. Gates foolishly agreed.

Gates was willing, even eager, to meet Cornwallis in formal battle in the open field, and on precisely such ground the two armies collided just north of Camden on August 16. The British had slightly more than 2,000 men, Gates about 3,000. The whole course of the war had shown that these were not the sort of odds which could produce an American success in head-on battle against veteran British troops.

Cornwallis's force amply qualified for that description:

three companies, 282 men, of the 23rd Regiment of Foot,
the Royal Welch Fuzileers; 283 men of the 33rd Regiment;
five companies, 237 men, of the 71st Highlanders; and some
of the quasi-regular Loyalist troops, 289 men of Tarleton's
Legion and 287 of Lord Rawdon's Volunteers of Ireland.
The bulk of the remainder consisted of two regiments of
North Carolina Loyalists; they may not have been up to the
standard of the others, but they were probably better than
Gates's militia. On the Revolutionary side, the Maryland
and Delaware Continentals numbered about 900 and were
among the few Continentals who had demonstrated a con-
sistent ability to stand up to the British no matter what the
kind of fighting; indeed, from the battle of Long Island in
1776 onward through the war, the Marylanders and Delawares seem to have been consistently the best of the Continental Army. But the rest of Gates's men in no way approached them. The rest were mainly Virginia and North
Carolina militia, citizens with a minimum of military training who had volunteered or, possibly though not likely, been
drafted for a term of service under the customary laws
which the states inherited from the colonial period, making
every able-bodied white male at least theoretically liable for
military service. Surveying the two armies, there was no
reason for Gates to expect he could win.

A familiar story tells how his defeat became more certain.
The night before the battle, some overdue provisions
reached Gates's army. The general turned even this development into misfortune by allowing his men time only to half-
cook their meat and half-bake their bread, following that
with a mixture of molasses and corn meal mush for dessert.
The dessert proved a powerful purgative. The men "were
breaking ranks all night and were certainly much debilitated
before the action commenced in the morning."

The Maryland and Delaware Continentals as usual fought

well, but Gates's militia panicked and fled the field—which
was not an unreasonable response to having to face a British
bayonet charge without bayonets and to the generalship they
had witnessed. So complete was the rout that only about
700 of Gates's army eventually rallied at Hillsborough. Gates
himself led the flight, riding sixty miles to Charlotte before
the day of battle ended and covering another 120 miles in
the next two days, a ride which "does admirable credit to
the activity of a man at his time of life," as Alexander
Hamilton remarked. De Kalb died with the Maryland and
Delaware Continentals, still leading them in a counterattack
after everyone else had fled.

If it were possible for British possession of South Carolina to be even more complete than after Lincoln's surrender
at Charleston, Gates's premature commitment of his army
to battle at Camden had obviously accomplished that result.
Two days afterward, furthermore, Tarleton surprised Sumter
in his camp at Fishing Creek, killed 150 of his men,
wounded 300, and recaptured the spoils of Sumter's raid on
Cornwallis's communications. When the news reached Eu-
rope, the Comte de Vergennes, foreign minister of France,
proposed peace with the British on the basis of *uti possidetis*
(the "state of possession"), to leave South Carolina perma-
nently in British hands.

Gamecock Sumter remained undiscourageable. He had
contributed his share to Gates's disaster, but he now re-
deemed himself by keeping the fight alive in spite of it.
Gathering followers anew, he repulsed a British cavalry
attack against his camp at Fish Dam Ford on the Broad
River. He next crossed the Broad to the westward to
threaten the far anchor of the British outpost system at
Ninety-Six. The British felt obliged to send Tarleton thither
to restrain him. On the way, Tarleton conducted his customary burnings, including Sumter's own mills which had

escaped him earlier. As a refinement in barbarity he ex-
humed the body of the recently deceased Colonel Richard
Richardson, the rebel leader of the early days of the war
in the upcountry.

On this occasion, unlike Fishing Creek, Sumter received
warning when Tarleton was approaching. He took up a
strong defensive position at Blackstocks Plantation, in a
bend of the Tyger River. With the rebels enjoying a sub-
stantial advantage in numbers and the enemy a similar advantage in military skill, they fought each other to a bloody
standoff, from which both sides withdrew at nightfall, both
making dubious claims of victory. Tarleton's claim was
diluted by his lament to Cornwallis: "But my Lord I have
lost men—50 killed & wounded & Officers which are losses
to the public Service." On the Revolutionary side, Sumter's
latest demonstration of his remarkable ability to rise and
fight again was spoiled by his suffering severe wounds of
the right shoulder, from which he never completely recovered though he lived to be ninety-eight. He was back in
the field in two and a half months, but his greatest days of
partisan leadership lay behind him.

By this time, fortunately for the rebels, another and in
some ways better partisan leader had risen from the coastal
swamps between the Pee Dee and the Santee to resume the
fight there, a leader better disciplined as well as a better
disciplinarian than Sumter, and much Sumter's superior in
ability both to plan ahead and to co-operate in others' plans.
This of course was Colonel Francis Marion. Some four
years older than Sumter, Marion had become a hero of the
province as early as 1761, when he led an important attack
as a lieutenant of William Moultrie's militia company in
Colonel James Grant's expedition against the Cherokee. He
gained renewed prominence in the defense of Charleston in
1776. He escaped capture in Lincoln's unsuccessful defense

through a strangely fortunate incident. Not long before the British invested the city, he jumped from a second story window to escape a drinking party he was not enjoying; in doing so he dislocated his ankle, so that he left the city to recuperate at his home in St. John's Parish. Recovered in time for the Camden campaign, Marion was welcomed back into the Revolutionary service by de Kalb; but the group of men who had followed him out of the swamps, black as well as white, looked so shaggy and disreputable that they became butts of humor among the Continentals, and consequently Gates rid himself of Marion and his disreputables by sending them off to watch the enemy in the upcountry.

Four days after the battle of Camden, Marion suggested how much Gates had lost in banishing him by attacking a British party that was escorting prisoners, at Great Savannah near Nelson's Ferry on the Santee. He rescued about 150 Maryland Continentals. Then he withdrew into the coastal lowlands to gather additional followers and raid the enemy's communications between Camden and the coast. He possessed a remarkable sense of direction and locale, and he knew intimately every byway of his coastal zone. Soon he was doing enough damage to draw Tarleton into action against him. That officer found chasing Marion through flooded bottomlands so futile and unpleasant a task that he gladly abandoned it to ride westward for the good cavalry roads of the upcountry, upon the expedition against Sumter which led to Blackstocks Plantation. "Come, my boys!" Tarleton is supposed to have said. "Let us go back and we will find the gamecock. But as for this damned old fox, the devil himself could not catch him!"

But no more than the Gamecock's were Swamp Fox Marion's operations likely by themselves to recapture South Carolina. Sumter and Marion probably could have kept both marshland and upcountry festering indefinitely, but probably also there would have come a time when the British wore them down. They could sour the fruits of Cornwallis's Camden victory, but the result of Camden remained: there was no solid core of rebel strength any-where in the Carolinas to prevent the British from dispers-ing enough to seek out and ultimately to subdue the partisans.

Without a solid rallying point, even so spectacular a rebel success as the battle of King's Mountain probably could have had no permanent effect. Major Patrick Fergu-son of the 71st Highlanders, who had gained notoriety with Tarleton at Monck's Corner, was now Cornwallis's inspector of militia, charged with organizing the armed Loyalists to keep rebels under control. After Camden, Cornwallis set out for the conquest of North Carolina, while Ferguson with varying numbers of his Loyalists ranged westward to assert the royal authority in the farther reaches of both Carolinas before rejoining Cornwallis somewhere in the north. For a time Ferguson was optimistic that the whole western coun-try was returning to its old allegiance, and he even threat-ened the settlements beyond the Appalachians that they had better make their peace or be punished. His very optimism and his threats convinced some of the leaders of the "over-mountain men" that they should do something to stop him, and they took the initiative in calling for a rendezvous of all the Revolutionary forces in the frontier districts. This call sent considerable numbers of over-mountain men east-ward, and it proved to rally still greater numbers from both Carolinas, all determined that Ferguson's pacification pro-gram had gone far enough.

Faced with superior numbers gathering against him, Ferguson began retreating eastward. But for some reason he soon decided to stop retreating and make a stand on King's Mountain, a wooded elevation which rises about sixty feet above the surrounding countryside. He must have thought that he could deal the rebels a signal setback; but he was curiously mistaken, especially so in view of the fact that he had a strong interest in rifles and had invented a superior rifled shoulder-arm. His Loyalists happened not to be armed with rifles. Many of the frontiersmen opposed to him, however, did have such weapons. When Ferguson halted on King's Mountain, his opponents were able to surround him. They then advanced up the hill from tree to tree, using their rifles to pick his men off. In the woods, the bayonet charges which Ferguson attempted as a counterstroke were futile. The rebels, between 1,400 and 1,800 of them, killed Ferguson and 157 of his Loyalists and captured the rest, 163 badly wounded and 698 others. Rebel firing went on long enough after Loyalist attempts to surrender to inspire the "Tarleton's quarter" kind of story, told now from the British and Loyalist side.

King's Mountain so stunned Cornwallis that he temporarily abandoned the march into North Carolina. The battle occurred on October 7, 1780, nearly simultaneous with Francis Marion's first major successes in beating up enemy outposts in the coastal swamps (Black Mingo, September 29, and Tearcoat Swamp, October 26), and just before Sumter's Fish Dam Ford-Blackstocks campaign (November 9–November 20). With the next problem for the Revolutionary forces in South Carolina being that of putting these pieces together into a coherent scheme of campaign, it was fortunate that also about the same time, on October 5, the Continental Congress voted to grant General Washington power to choose a successor to Gates in the southern command. Washington selected the officer he had recommended in the first place, before Gates's disaster, Major General Nathanael Greene of Rhode Island. On December 2, Greene arrived at Charlotte to take the reins from

Gates. As events were about to demonstrate, the still barely
surviving rebel cause in the South thus passed into the
hands of perhaps the best qualified to restore it of all
generals in American history, our most successful master
of the art of nourishing irregular war into complete military
triumph.

Cowpens: December 2, 1780–January 17, 1781

"Guerrilla war, too, inverts one of the main principles of orthodox
war, the principle of 'concentration'—and on both sides."
—B. H. Liddell Hart, *Strategy*

Greene forthwith demonstrated his perception—which
Gates had lacked—that the southern campaign could no
longer be fought according to the ordinary principles of
war, that the Revolutionary forces were too weak for that.
The usual understanding of the principles of war would have
led him to keep whatever main force he could muster closed
up and well in hand, on the assumption that this force must
strike the decisive blow if there was to be one and that it
must be concentrated for that purpose; this idea is what
modern textbooks call the principle of mass, or the principle
of concentration.

Greene, however, knew that no force he could muster
could hope to stand successfully against the concentrated
army of the enemy. Therefore he boldly proceeded to divide
his small main body into two smaller fragments, taking the
gamble that he would thus lead the enemy to divide himself
too into pieces small enough to deal with. But he did
retain two recognizable principal forces, even though they
were small for that purpose, because he wanted to pose

enough of a threat of concentrated power to prevent Cornwallis from dispersing so freely that the British could menace all the guerrilla bands. Greene was going to tread a very thin line between excessive concentration and excessive dispersion, and to run grave risks that the enemy might destroy one or both of his two principal forces in the process. But running risks is a necessity if weak forces are to achieve great objects.

Specifically, Greene found that at Hillsborough Gates had rallied from the Camden disaster a force counted on its muster rolls as 2,457 strong, though with only 1,482 present and fit for duty, only 1,099 of the muster-roll strength Continentals, and all "wretched beyond description, and their distress, on account of [lack of] provisions, was little less than their suffering for want of clothing and other necessaries." Three days' provisions were on hand, with nothing more on the horizon.

Greene forthwith sent the Polish engineer Thaddeus Kosciuszko to find a reasonably secure place in a district fruitful enough for the army to refit, and Kosciuszko chose the Cheraw Hill area just below the border between the two Carolinas, a place of rebel sentiment on the Pee Dee River. Greene marched there with most of his little force. But he promptly dispatched Brigadier General Daniel Morgan with a detachment of 600 westward towards Ninety-Six, with orders to conduct himself "either offensively or defensively, as your own prudence and discretion may direct—acting with caution and avoiding surprises by every possible precaution." When Lieutenant Colonel Henry Lee—"Light Horse Harry"—arrived presently from the North at the head of his Legion of 100 horse and 180 foot, Greene similarly detached him to co-operate with Marion in operations against Georgetown on the coast.

Dividing the army would make it easier for all the parts

of it to find enough to eat, but important as that consideration was, it was not the principal reason for the division.
Greene's stratagem was intended to complicate Cornwallis's
apparent intent to renew the invasion of North Carolina.
Cornwallis and Tarleton, who had become the British commander's close friend and confidant, could hardly believe
what was happening, so inconsistent with the acknowledged
customs of civilized war was Greene's division of his inferior force. Tarleton therefore urged a rapid strike against
Greene while Morgan was absent. But Cornwallis could
recognize by now how little it had profited him to destroy
or nearly destroy two successive Revolutionary armies,
Lincoln's and Gates's. A similar exploit against Greene
would hardly accomplish more, if Morgan should take the
opportunity to capture Ninety-Six and thus follow up King's
Mountain by raising the whole western area to arms again.
If Cornwallis's whole force moved against Morgan, however,
then Greene would be in a position to threaten Charleston.
Therefore, Cornwallis divided his own force, sending a
disapproving Tarleton with about 1,100 men, mixed cavalry
and infantry, as was now customary for long forays into the
interior, to deal with Morgan preliminary to a major effort
against Greene. "Col. Tarleton is said to be on his way to
pay you a visit," Greene wrote to Morgan. "I doubt not but
he will have a decent reception and a proper dismission."

Morgan gathered militia to augment his detachment to
about 1,040 men. They were of the usual varied quality but
included some 320 of the stout Maryland and Delaware
Continentals and 60 to 100 Continental light dragoons, who
could fight either mounted or on foot, under William Washington. Dan Morgan of Virginia had been famous almost
since he first led his company of riflemen into George
Washington's camps at Cambridge at the beginning of the
war, and he had assured the permanence of his fame by his

leadership on Benedict Arnold's march to Quebec and by
his handling of a rifle corps in the decisive moments at
Bemis Heights and Freeman's Farm in the Saratoga campaign. After that, however, he had gone home in disgust
when Washington gave the elite light infantry corps of the
main army not to him but to the less proven Anthony
Wayne. Gates then persuaded Morgan to join the southern
army to restore their Saratoga partnership, but sciatica kept
him away until after Camden.

Morgan was as pugnacious as Gamecock Sumter. When
he learned that Tarleton had crossed the Tyger River and
was approaching his position on the Pacolet, he wrote to
Greene: "My force is inadequate to the attempts you have
hinted at." But then he turned to offer battle anyway, in a
place not well chosen, apparently out of sheer impatience
for a fight. After Tarleton had outmaneuvered him to get
across the Pacolet, Morgan began retreating towards the
Broad River as though to cross it ahead of the enemy. Then
instead he turned to make a stand with the Broad behind
him, at a place where a prosperous Loyalist named Hiram
Saunders had been accustomed to rounding up his cattle,
therefore called the Cowpens.

The wisdom of Morgan's decision to fight is highly
debatable. On the face of it, if Gates was wrong to offer
battle at Camden, Morgan was equally wrong at the Cowpens, for the same reasons. It may be that Tarleton was
closing up so rapidly that Morgan thought he had no choice
but to stand. If so, he might still have found a better loca-
tion. At the Cowpens the Broad River would cut off his
retreat if he was beaten, and the field was a generally open
one with scattered pines, chestnut, and oak but with no
underbrush, excellent ground for Tarleton's more numerous
cavalry and without anchors for Morgan's flanks. Morgan
later rationalized his choice of place by writing that he did

not want to have a line of retreat; his militia would fight
much better if they knew they could not flee. In fact, however, only two considerations can absolve Morgan from the
charge of repeating the mistakes Gates made before Camden. First, Morgan may have judged Tarleton to be an over-
rated officer who had never before held independent command against good American fighters ably led. Second,
Morgan felt confidence born of experience that he himself
was a first-rate tactician and an inspiring battle captain,
who could overcome the deficiencies both of the battle-
ground and of his men. The clincher is that he was right.

He chose to place his militia, about 300 men from both
the Carolinas, under Colonel Andrew Pickens of Long Cane
Creek, about 150 yards in advance of his main line. Still
farther in front were about 150 picked riflemen, Georgians
and North Carolinians. The main line, at the crest of a
gentle slope, consisted of the Maryland and Delaware Continentals under Lieutenant Colonel John Eager Howard,
plus some Virginia and a few Georgia militiamen who happened to be mainly discharged Continentals. Morgan's in-
structions were that when Tarleton attacked, the sharpshooters were to do as much damage as they could, aiming for
officers. They were then to fall back into the Carolina
militia line, which was to fire deliberately until hard pressed
and then to retreat by the left flank to a place shielded by
hills behind the main line. Repeatedly in earlier battles,
inexperienced militia had ruined everything for the Revolutionaries by fleeing the field. Now Morgan included their
predictable retreat in his plans, carefully explaining everything to them, allowing them to keep their horses tethered
at the designated destination of their retreat in case they
should have to pull back farther, but assuring them that
they and the sharpshooters would inflict enough punishment before the British hit the main line that there was

no need to fear the main line would not hold. Meanwhile William Washington's dragoons and Lieutenant Colonel James McCall's Georgia mounted infantry would serve as a reserve and might cover the flanks. Morgan's plan was unorthodox for its time, but modern readers will recognize it as a well calculated defense in depth.

Morgan in person explained these details to his men as he roamed among them during the night before the battle, reminding them also of the plundering of their homes by British and Loyalists, and reputedly displaying his own scars received when the British army sentenced him to a whipping for striking a British officer during the French and Indian War. Next day, he said, "Old Wagoner" Morgan would apply the whip to Ban Tarleton.

When Tarleton's force arrived at the Cowpens in the morning of January 17, 1781, already weary from a five-hour march, Morgan's line of sharpshooters prevented any adequate reconnaissance of his positions. When Tarleton ordered the cavalry of his Legion to drive away the sharpshooters, the riflemen drove back the cavalry instead. Then the riflemen retired into the militia line as instructed. The militia too fired deliberately as instructed, when Tarleton sent his main line of infantry forward, light infantry of various regiments on the left, infantry of Tarleton's Legion in the center, and a battalion of the 7th Royal English Fuzileers on the right. Most of Pickens's militiamen got off two well aimed shots; the enemy faltered but then came on again. The militia then retreated. British cavalry tried to break up their movement, but Washington and McCall intervened, and the retreat proceeded as planned.

Morgan's main line was also fighting as planned when Tarleton extended his line to the left by throwing in his reserve, a battalion of the 71st Highlanders. Tarleton's line then outreached Morgan's, and in the effort to adjust

the American right accordingly, there occurred a confusion
of orders which precipitated a general retreat. This of
course was not part of the plan; but it was an orderly
retreat, not a rout, and the British line began to lose
its cohesion as Tarleton's soldiers came on excitedly, assuming the day was won. Washington told Morgan the
enemy was becoming so disorganized that if the infantry
would turn and give them one fire, he would charge them.
At this juncture Pickens's militiamen, still well in hand,
came up on Morgan's right. Morgan ordered the one fire,
his infantry turned and obeyed, Howard ordered the Continental infantry to countercharge with the bayonet, and the
Revolutionary cavalry rode into the enemy's flanks and rear.
Except for the Highlanders, Tarleton's men fled the field
or surrendered, some Revolutionary officers finding difficulty in restraining their men from granting "Tarleton's
quarter." The Highlanders gave way only when the whole
rebel force concentrated upon them.

Never before in the war had a Revolutionary army won
so complete a tactical victory over an opposing force made
up largely of British regulars. Nine-tenths of Tarleton's
detachment were killed or captured, along with their two
three-pounder cannon and most of their baggage and ammunition. Morgan lost only twelve killed and sixty wounded.
South Carolina made Andrew Pickens a brigadier. The
stimulus to Revolutionary morale all over the South could
not but be immense.

But the material weight of Greene's forces remained
as inferior to Cornwallis's as before; Major General Alexander Leslie had just joined Cornwallis with 1,500 men
from Clinton's northern British army. The Revolutionary
position remained therefore nearly as precarious as ever.
Cornwallis at length had decided that he could not free his
mind to deal properly with Greene until Morgan was dis-

posed of and he had been bringing up his main body in
Tarleton's support, whatever the risks to Charleston. It must
be said in Tarleton's behalf that if Cornwallis had been
where Tarleton urged him to be on the day of Cowpens, he
would have stood at King's Mountain in Morgan's rear, bar-
ring Morgan's withdrawal towards Greene. Nervousness
about Greene's force on his right flank had delayed Cornwallis's advance, thus rendering still another dividend for
Greene's division of his forces. Nevertheless, Cornwallis
was at Turkey Creek only thirty miles from the Cowpens
on the day of the battle, and Morgan knew he would have
the news from Tarleton's survivors within a few hours.
Morgan felt he must see to the wounded of his own and
Tarleton's force, and he had the encumbrance of prisoners
two-thirds as numerous as his own men. Three rivers, the
Broad, the Catawba, and the Pee Dee, lay between him and
whatever protection Greene's main force could afford him.
The road to a juncture with Greene led through Ramsour's
Mills, a place no closer to the Cowpens than to Cornwallis
at Turkey Creek, whence another road reached it. Thus
Morgan remained in grave danger of entrapment by a
British force much bigger and much better led than Tarle-
ton's. He must flee, if he could.

The Race to the Dan: January 17–February 14, 1781

"The ability to run away is the very characteristic of the guerrilla."
—Mao Tse-tung

Cornwallis had enough experience with the peculiarities
of revolutionary war in America to know that even the
destruction of a rebel army might be followed merely by

the rising of another; but he knew too that if partisan war against British authority were ever to cease, Greene's army must first be destroyed to deny the partisans their rallying point. Perhaps more compelling than that thought, Greene's army was also an objective with which Cornwallis knew how to cope in the terms of conventional European military principles. Time and again in unconventional wars, the forces engaged in suppressing guerrillas have tried almost compulsively to goad the enemy into pitched battle, into an action both comprehensible to them and perhaps altogether destructive to the enemy. Not infrequently, that understandable compulsiveness has brought disaster not to the guerrillas but to the conventional army, because compulsive behavior implies irrationality and desperation which can be exploited. The most notable example in recent history is that of the French in Indochina in 1954, whose urgent longing for a set-piece engagement brought on the battle of Dienbienphu. Cornwallis, similarly compulsive, was about to set his army on a path to similar disaster.

Cornwallis was an intelligent soldier and the most enterprising commander to lead a British army in the whole course of the American Rebellion. It is another example of the way in which irregular war inverts the norms of orthodox war and sets snares even for the best practitioners of conventional campaigning that the enterprising Cornwallis now plunged into difficulties which a sluggish officer such as Sir Henry Clinton would have avoided. When he learned of Cowpens, Cornwallis became determined both that Morgan's escape from destruction should be temporary, and that if possible he would not only run Morgan to ground but use the occasion to bring Greene himself to battle when Greene tried to protect Morgan.

Unfortunately for his purpose, Cornwallis began by misjudging Morgan, assuming that the Virginian would be so

puffed up by his Cowpens victory that he would remain
complacently in the neighborhood. Therefore Cornwallis
moved first towards the battlefield rather than to Ramsour's
Mills where he might have cut off Morgan's retreat. By the
time he discovered his error and arrived at Ramsour's Mills,
Morgan was two days gone. Disgusted, Cornwallis decided
upon drastic remedies to permit him to march faster than
the rebels and thus force them to battle.

He spent two days at Ramsour's Mills burning all his
provisions, except such as the men could carry in their
haversacks, all his tents, and all his wagons except the
barest minimum needed to transport ammunition, salt, and
hospital stores plus four for the sick and wounded. Even
his army's liquor he poured away. Then he set out on
January 27, unencumbered enough to track the rebels in
one of the most rapid marches of military history.

Dan Morgan, too shrewd for complacency after Cowpens,
had put the Broad River between himself and the enemy
before January 17 was over. By the time Cornwallis moved
on from Ramsour's Mills, he was not only across the Catawba
but had disposed of the Cowpens prisoners by detaching
Pickens to Island Ford up the river, where Pickens turned
the prisoners over to a Continental commissary of prisoners
who led them into Virginia. Meanwhile news of the situation, including the Cowpens victory, had reached Greene at
Cheraw. Recognizing Morgan's peril, Greene ordered Isaac
Huger to lead the main army up the Pee Dee and the
Yadkin—they are the same river—to try to rendezvous with
Morgan in North Carolina. Greene himself with a small
escort rode cross-country to join Morgan and concert plans.

From the time of his advance to Cheraw, Greene had
reckoned with the possibility that the inferiority of his
army to Cornwallis's might compel a hasty retreat. Therefore he had dispatched his quartermaster, Lieutenant

Colonel Edward Carrington, to explore and map the crossings of the Dan River far in his rear, and Kosciuszko and
Major General Edward Stevens of the Virginia militia to
do the same for the crossings of the Catawba and the
Yadkin. All were to collect and build flatboats to cross the
rivers, boats capable of being carried on wheels or wagons
from one river to another. When he sent Huger up the
Yadkin, Greene directed Carrington back to the Dan to
complete the assembly of the boats. When Greene arrived
at Morgan's camp, Morgan proposed a retreat westward
into the mountains, where Cornwallis's army could not follow. But Greene learned from Morgan that Cornwallis had
destroyed his own baggage and was pressing the pursuit.
"Then, he is ours!" Greene is supposed to have exclaimed.
He proposed to retreat not where Cornwallis could not
follow but where he could follow, luring Cornwallis farther
and farther northward on a march so long that the absence
of his baggage would exhaust and ruin him.

But Cornwallis was marching fast, with almost 3,000
men, and he must not catch Morgan's detachment before it
reunited with Huger's. Therefore Greene ordered Brigadier
General William Lee Davidson of the North Carolina militia
to use his men in delaying Cornwallis at the crossings of
the Catawba while Morgan resumed the retreat. Once again
the part-time soldiery of the militia gave the Revolutionary
forces a flexibility of infinite value. Davidson obstructed
some of the Catawba fords with felled trees and prepared
to contest others. The main action took place at Cowan's
Ford in the early morning of February 1. Troops from the
so-called Brigade of Guards, drawn from the 23rd, 33rd, and
71st Regiments and all excellent professional soldiers, spear-
headed the British crossing. Despite their taking the deep
wagon ford rather than the path they should have used—
because their guide ran away from them—the Guards got

over the river. In the ensuing skirmish General Davidson fell dead, and his militia then scattered. But because the militia had been available to impose about as much delay as could be hoped for, Morgan was thirty miles distant.

Greene was not; he was waiting for the militia to rendezvous and escape. At Tarrant's Tavern, however, some ten miles beyond the river, Tarleton came riding into the militia as they tried to reassemble and quickly broke them up. Greene was just a short distance farther on and lucky not to be captured. At length he resumed a solitary retreat.

Morgan passed through Salisbury, North Carolina and reached the Yadkin at Trading Ford the next day, February 2. He found it swelled beyond its normal fording depth by heavy rains, but fortunately Kosciuszko had seen to it that boats were there. The Americans crossed during the night, and when the British advance guard, still pressing forward with remarkable energy, arrived on the 3rd, the deep river stymied them. They had to content themselves with a halfhearted artillery bombardment.

Cornwallis learned that Shallow Ford, ten miles up the Yadkin, was always fordable, and he swung westward to use it. This shift away from Greene seemed a reasonable movement because Cornwallis also had information that the rains had made the lower Dan River fords impassable, that in the winter season they were likely to remain so, and that Greene did not have enough boats on the Dan to be ferried across before Cornwallis could hit him; therefore Greene too would have to shift westward to reach the upper fords of the Dan, and Cornwallis's movement would give the British an advantageous position. In fact, the crossing of the Dan was another contingency for which Greene had thoroughly prepared. For a time the American commander marched directly northward from Trading Ford, encouraging Cornwallis in his conviction that the rebels would have

to go to the upper Dan. Near Salem, however, Greene
turned eastward, to reunite at last with Huger's force at
Guilford Court House. Huger too had arrived after a march
of great difficulty, for the hard and steady rains had made
an appalling mess of the clay roads, and many of his men
had long since worn out their shoes.

Briefly Greene considered standing at Guilford Court
House, to give Cornwallis the battle he wanted. Greene had
ordered Lee's Legion up from the lower Pee Dee, and Lee
was with Huger. Still, Greene's reunited forces numbered
barely 2,000, and fewer than 1,500 were Continentals who
could be relied upon in the open field. Cornwallis's hard
march was already dropping men behind it, but the enemy
must still have had at least 2,500 first-rate troops. Few
militia were joining Greene. A council of war therefore
decided not to fight, but to continue the retreat to Boyd's
and Irwin's ferries on the lower Dan. To make life as difficult as possible for Cornwallis, Greene sent General Pickens
back to try to raise militia from South Carolina and to in-
terfere with the enemy's provisioning himself.

To hold Cornwallis at arm's length during the final
plunge of seventy or so miles to the Dan, and to march over
roads which would maintain the impression that the destination was the upper fords, Greene detached 700 of his best
men as a rear guard, including a battalion of 280 Continental
infantry under Colonel Howard; all the cavalry, both William Washington's and Lee's Legion; and sixty Virginia
riflemen. Morgan was offered this command but declined,
perhaps as he said because his back pains were returning,
perhaps because with his idea of a retreat to the mountains
rejected he thought the whole enterprise too risky, more
likely for both reasons. The command then went to Colonel
Otho Holland Williams, outstanding among the many able

officers produced by the Maryland Continentals. Morgan left the field never to return.

Greene struck out from Guilford for the Dan on February 10. That day Cornwallis was leaving Salem, not far behind. In the next few days Cornwallis moved as much as thirty miles a day, a stupendous feat over clay roads still badly broken up by the rains and alternately freezing by night and thawing by day. Otho Williams had to march just as fast to stay ahead of him, while Williams's horsemen patrolled constantly to hold off enemy forays and make sure that none of the British slipped between the rear guard and Greene's main body. This activity was possible because the American cavalry, drawing on nearby Virginia, now had sturdier and faster mounts than the overstrained horses of the British. Still, Williams felt obliged to keep half his cavalry patrolling all night long, which meant that the troopers got only six hours sleep out of every forty-eight.

Tarleton, an able cavalryman whatever his shortcomings in independent command, discerned the true direction of Greene's march and reported accordingly to Cornwallis before dawn on February 13. Cornwallis promptly shifted eastward, nearly crashing unannounced into Henry Lee's rear of the rear guard while they relaxed over their one daily meal. Rescued from his unaccustomed lack of vigilance by the warnings of a countryman, Lee formed ranks in time for an unpleasant clash with Tarleton, marred by the alleged cold-blooded murder of Lee's unarmed, teen-aged bugler. The pace then quickened still more, as Cornwallis now pushed on with the energy of desperation to catch the rebels before they reached the boats which he had to surmise were awaiting them on the Dan. For a second time in the day, Lee's men were interrupted while trying to enjoy their daily repast, as Cornwallis's vanguard pressed close upon them.

The roads remained rough, the creeks swollen. Repeatedly the British van came within musket shot of the American rear, and repeatedly it seemed that Lee and Williams must turn and fight. As they approached a line of glowing campfires, the rear guard feared Greene himself had been unable to cross and had halted for a last stand. But the fires proved to be burning as a welcome and a reassurance, accompanied by a message from Greene that his baggage was crossing the Dan and the main body would soon follow.

The Dan was still forty miles from the campfires, and after a rest of two or three hours near the fires Cornwallis drove his men forward to march those last forty miles in twenty-four hours. But Williams's men covered the same distance in sixteen hours, and all the Americans got across the river. Colonel Carrington, whose careful labors made the escape possible, accompanied Henry Lee in the last boat, about midnight of February 14. The British advance reached the south shore almost as soon as the two colonels landed on the north, but the river was indeed too deep to ford, and the boats were all with the rebels.

So Cornwallis stood on the south shore with an exhausted army stripped of its means of sustenance, while Colonel Pickens with 700 Revolutionary militia scoured the country-side in his rear. For Greene, Virginia was no land of milk and honey; it had its own problems and was suffering its own depredations at the hands of British and Loyalist raiders. But there was enough for limited foraging and replenishment, and Baron von Steuben was raising Continental recruits. If Cornwallis should summon up an incredible further exertion to cross the Dan, Greene could fall back upon Steuben and the British would be outnumbered substantially. In fact, Cornwallis was at the end of his tether; he would make no crossing. His forced march on short rations had already cost him 500 men since Ramsour's Mills, sick and deserters, and he saw nothing to do but retreat to Hillsborough, there to try to regather his strength, and to proclaim the return of North Carolina to the Crown. His proclamation would be less well received because of the plundering which his jettisoning of his baggage had helped occasion along his line of march.

Nevertheless, the proclamation was a sore point for the Revolutionaries. Greene had won a kind of victory in the race to the Dan, but now North as well as South Carolina again flew the royal standard.

Guilford Court House and Greene's Return to South Carolina: February 14–April 5, 1781

". . . enemy advances, we retreat; enemy halts, we harass; enemy tires, we attack; enemy retreats, we pursue."

—Mao Tse-tung

Running away could never accomplish more than such negative successes, while Greene's purpose was the positive one of restoring the Revolution in both Carolinas. Though Greene would deny Cornwallis's thirst for battle as long as Cornwallis was sure to win, he knew that to win himself he must soon turn from running to strike. As soon as Cornwallis withdrew from the Dan River, Greene sent Lee's Legion and two companies of Maryland Continentals back to the southern shore to join Picken's campaign of harassment. Two days later the rest of Otho Williams's force followed. On February 23, as soon as he was joined by General Stevens with 600 Virginia militia, Greene himself re-entered North Carolina. He believed Cornwallis had so

badly overextended himself that the time to fight had almost arrived.

Sharing Greene's now aggressive mood, Pickens and Lee
tried to bring Tarleton to combat. They failed, coming into
one of his camps just after he had vacated it. In the process,
however, they captured two of his staff officers, and Lee
then conceived the idea that with the two officers as decoys,
he would lure local Loyalists into the Revolutionaries' net
by pretending to be Tarleton himself. Such a deception
seemed possible because both Lee's and Tarleton's legion-
aries wore forest green uniforms.

The idea succeeded beyond expectations. With the
British officers conspicuously present, Lee encountered two
young farmers who received the impression that he was Tarleton and told him they were being followed by 400 Loyalist
recruits on their way to join Tarleton's command. Lee
assured them that indeed he was Tarleton and sent them
back to their leader, a Colonel John Pyle, to tell him to
draw his men up for inspection. Sending word to Pickens
to follow with his militia and conceal himself in woods,
Lee led his cavalry in single file, with drawn sabres, past
Pyle's recruits as though reviewing them. He said in his
memoirs that as soon as he was sure the recruits were all at
his mercy he intended to reveal his true identity and order
Pyle to surrender. At the moment when according to his
account he was about to do that, however, some of the
Loyalists saw and recognized Pickens's militia in the woods.
The Loyalists opened fire on Captain Joseph Eggleston's
company of Lee's Legion, Eggleston immediately ordered
his men into action, Lee followed suit, and a slaughter of
the Loyalists took place. The range and the warning were
both too short for the Loyalists to defend themselves with
their muskets and rifles against drawn sabres. Ninety of

them were killed, most of the rest wounded, including Pyle, and not a man of Lee's was injured.

This affair at Haw River dried up Loyalist recruiting in North Carolina. Meanwhile Cornwallis's forced requisitions of foodstuffs were doing the British no good in the sympathies of the Hillsborough area. Cornwallis thought it advisable to move again, both to find other provisioning grounds and in the long deferred hope of punishing the rebels. At Clapp's Mills on March 2 and Wetzell's Mills on March 6, Cornwallis's vanguard tangled with Otho Williams's troops, hoping to draw Greene's main body into action. On both occasions the Revolutionaries were able to frustrate this intent. But Greene did not propose to frustrate it much longer. He received 400 Continental recruits from Steuben in Virginia, plus 1,060 North Carolina and 1,693 Virginia militia. He was never likely to be much stronger, and like his adversary he was finding provisioning in North Carolina increasingly difficult. On March 14 he halted his movements at a defensive position at Guilford Court House, the ground where he had been tempted to fight in February. He was ready to oblige Cornwallis.

British historians are apt to make much of the heavy numerical superiority which Greene now enjoyed over Cornwallis, probably some 4,400 troops to about 1,900. American writers are more likely to point out, as Henry Lee did in his memoirs, that among Greene's infantry only one regiment of Maryland Continentals, a company of Delawares, and the foot soldiers of Lee's Legion, perhaps 500 in all, could be counted as disciplined veterans, while nearly all of Cornwallis's men fit into that category. Notwithstanding the happy exception to the rule at Cowpens, Greene's numerical superiority was about what experience indicated was necessary for a good chance of winning.

At least as important is the consideration recognized

by Tarleton, that Greene had waited to give battle only at
the moment most propitious for him: "A defeat of the
British," Tarleton said, "could have been attended with the
total destruction of Earl Cornwallis's infantry, while a victory at this juncture could produce no very decisive conse-
quences against the Americans." Cornwallis's army, driven
to the limits of endurance by the march to the Dan and its
inability fully to restore the provisions it had destroyed
at Ramsour's Mills, might well collapse altogether if it met
defeat. Even tactical victory by a narrow margin could
accomplish little more than to push it still further towards
utter exhaustion. Its weakened condition, and the mass if
not the quality of the Americans, assured that no greater
victory could await it. But Cornwallis would not be the last
commander who, infuriated by his inability to reduce revolutionary war to familiar and manageable dimensions, would
resort at last to a set-piece battle because it seemed the only
card left for him to play. So intent upon battle was he that
he plunged his men into it with empty stomachs after a
twelve-hour approach march.

The battle of Guilford Court House on March 15 permitted Greene to redeem South Carolina, but it is not
directly an event of South Carolina history, and the details
of its tactics need not be recapitulated here. Unlike Gates
at Camden, Greene chose a field studded here and there
with trees, to break up British alignments. He used a plan
similar to Morgan's at Cowpens, drawing up his men on a
gentle slope with the militia in advance, under orders to
fire and then to withdraw. Events did not turn out so well
for Greene as they had for Morgan, partly because most of
the North Carolina militia who formed the first line ran
away in disorder after firing their two volleys and did not
reform, more because Greene had to be more cautious than
Morgan about throwing everything he had into a climactic

counterattack, since unlike Morgan he had no larger force
waiting in the wings to back him up. The Virginia militia
fought well and the Continentals superbly, the latter standing up to Cornwallis's Guards in the most desperate close-
order fighting, until Cornwallis fired grapeshotted artillery
indiscriminately into the mass of Guards and Continentals.
If Greene had counterattacked at this moment, he probably
would have won a victory greater than Morgan's. But rather
than run undue risks with the whole of the regular forces
in the South, he retreated.

Cornwallis held the battlefield. For this traditional sym-
bol of victory he paid with some 532 casualties, including
ninety-three killed in action and fifty found dead of wounds
on the field next day—dead of wounds which would not
usually have been mortal, except that the British army was
too tired to tend to them quickly. Lee placed the American
casualties at 326 killed, wounded, and missing. Cornwallis's
losses were more than he could afford. All he could give
his men to eat after the battle were four ounces of flour and
four ounces of lean beef apiece. With militia all around
him, he could not detach parties to forage for more, even
had the countryside held more to find. He could not fight
another battle, for to duplicate the losses of Guilford would
ruin him completely. After two days' rest on the battlefield,
he retreated to the Cape Fear River. When Greene turned
to follow, the British moved downriver to Wilmington, the
ocean, and supplies. Thereupon Greene wrote to Washington: "I am determined to carry the war immediately into
South Carolina." He marched on April 5.

The Conquest of the British Garrisons:
April 5–June 5, 1781

"The chief problem . . . [was] the eternal one of military posts
and their combination with mobile columns. If the posts were suffi-
ciently strong and situated where they could be readily supplied and
reinforced, the distance between them permitted deep and sudden
penetration. If they were unduly weak, they were easily overwhelmed."
                                        —Cyril Falls, *A Hundred Years of War*
                                        (commenting on the Riff War of the 1920's)

The race to the Dan and the battle of Guilford Court
House bore closely upon the struggle for South Carolina
because they came near to reversing the military situation
created in that state by Lincoln's surrender at Charleston
and the battle of Camden. The latter two events had destroyed the main body of Revolutionary forces in the state,
leaving no center of resistance upon which irregulars might
rally. The race to the Dan and Guilford Court House now
left the British and Loyalists in South Carolina in the same
predicament—fighting without the main body of their army
as an anchor of security for their smaller detachments. For
Cornwallis was so close to ruin that he decided he dared
not resume campaigning in the Carolinas, and he departed
from the arena.

When Greene resolved to return to South Carolina, his
first object was to co-operate with the partisans in gobbling
up the garrisoned posts with which the British sought to
make their strength felt throughout the state. He detached
Lee to reunite with Marion and attack Fort Watson on the
Santee. He urged Pickens to operate against Ninety-Six. He

himself would march upon Gates's old objective, the central and crucial British post at Camden.

Cornwallis decided not to follow, but to transfer his campaign to Virginia. He persuaded himself that at Wilmington he was too far from Camden to intervene there before the course of events was determined anyway. If the troops in the neighborhood could turn back Greene, Cornwallis would not be needed; if they could not, he would be too late. More than that, Cornwallis regarded a return to the interior of the Carolinas as suicidal. He would move instead to Virginia, where deep tidal estuaries penetrated far inland and, he hoped, he need never be far distant from British sea power. Here too, he told himself, lay the true seat of Revolution in the South, so that triumph in Virginia would cause both Carolinas to fall readily into his arms. The beauty of Nathanael Greene's strategy was that with Cornwallis brought to so sorry a pass that he removed himself from the board, nothing now could prevent Greene and the partisans from eliminating the British garrisons in South Carolina one by one, as inexorably and inevitably as the unfolding of a theorem in geometry.

It is true that even with Cornwallis's departure some 8,000 British and Loyalist troops remained in South Carolina. Their ranking field commander, Lieutenant Colonel Francis Lord Rawdon, was willing to abandon posts and consolidate troops to create a new field army, and obviously he had enough men to build a very formidable one. But the guerrilla risings of Sumter, Marion, Pickens, and others had caused the British to spread themselves too thin. Before Rawdon could gather in the garrisons, the rebels were upon them. Because Greene and the partisans could choose the pattern of their attacks, they could always bring superior force against a given post. Because the partisan war had already progressed so far that the countryside generally belonged to the Revolutionaries, it was not unusual when Rawdon's orders to abandon posts and consolidate miscarried.

Lee and Marion began against Fort Watson because its capture would impair British communications between Charleston and Greene's own target of Camden. Sumter had already had a go at Watson in February, a botched attack undertaken without reconnaissance in a botched campaign which Greene had tried to forestall, and whose principal result was to augment the brutalization of the war. "A few days ago," wrote Lieutenant Colonel John W. T. Watson, for whom the British post was named, "after Genl. Sumter had taken some waggons on the other side of the Santee, and the escort of them had laid down their arms, a party of his horse who said they had not discharged their pieces came up, fired upon the prisoners and killed seven of them. A few days after we took six of his people. Enquire how they were treated."

When Lee and Marion arrived at Fort Watson on April 15, Watson himself and most of the garrison, some 500 men from elite "flank companies" of light infantry and grenadiers, were beating through the Pee Dee swamps in search of Marion. The remaining defenders were only eighty British regulars and forty Loyalists. Still, the stockade walls were strong, and three rows of abatis surrounded them. The fort commanded a level plain from atop an Indian mound. Lee and Marion had no artillery and no entrenching tools, and they had to get results quickly lest Watson return from the swamps. Therefore Colonel Hezekiah Maham proposed the building of a log tower tall enough to permit firing downward into the interior of the fort. The commanders told him to build it, and he did so, prefabricating the logs and then assembling them within rifle shot of the fort on the night of April 22. A party of riflemen began firing from the top of Maham's tower at dawn. When two other parties attacked the abatis, the defenders were unable to fight them without exposing themselves to the tower. Fort Watson surrendered.

Meanwhile, on April 19 Greene arrived in the vicinity of Camden. This post was one of the few in which the British had retained fairly large numbers; Greene faced about 900 British and Loyalists under Lord Rawdon himself. Rawdon was only twenty-seven years old, but he had campaigned in America since Bunker Hill, and he was highly capable.

As Greene approached, he received information that Colonel Watson's force was marching to strengthen Rawdon, and Greene maneuvered to try to prevent a juncture. Because he had to cross a difficult natural obstacle, steep-sided Pine Tree Creek, Greene sent his three six-pounder artillery pieces twenty miles to the rear, along with his baggage, for safekeeping. He then learned that Lee and Marion had moved from Fort Watson to block Colonel Watson's approach, and accordingly he shifted again to a position from which to threaten Camden, a sandy ridge called Hobkirk's Hill about a mile and a half north of the town. His 1,400 or so men, however, were not enough to assault good defensive works held by Rawdon's force, so he settled down to await reinforcements from Sumter, Marion, and Lee. The latter two were still busy with Watson; Sumter ignored Greene's appeals to join him. At this juncture Rawdon heard that Greene had sent his artillery away, and he decided to seize the initiative. On April 25 he moved against Greene with parts of one British and three Loyalist regiments, the 63rd, his own Volunteers of Ireland, the New York Volunteers, and the King's American Regiment, plus sixty New York dragoons and a small party of South Carolina Loyalist militia.

It happened that Greene's artillery had rejoined him,

but Rawdon's advance still gave the British the advantage of surprise. The pine woods and the terrain at Hobkirk's Hill were such that Greene's men could not see a force approaching from Camden until it was almost upon them, and Rawdon drove in Greene's pickets and then Captain Robert Kirkwood's company of Delaware Continentals. The Delawares fought with their customary bravery, holding their ground until Rawdon brought all of his light infantry upon them. Their stand permitted Greene to turn out his main body and try to grasp control of the situation.

Once he had disposed of the pickets and Kirkwood, Rawdon deployed on a rather narrow front for the attack upon Hobkirk's Hill, with the King's Americans, the New York Volunteers, and the 63rd Regiment from left to right in his front and his other units in support. Greene concluded that the narrowness of Rawdon's front permitted him to regain the initiative; he opened with a discharge from his artillery, then sent forward the First Maryland and Fifth Virginia Continentals in his center, with the Fifth Maryland and Fourth Virginia on his left and right flanks and instructed to close around Rawdon's flanks in a double envelopment. Otho Williams commanded Greene's left, Isaac Huger his right.

Rawdon responded by bringing up his reserves to extend his own line until it in turn overlapped Greene's; the Volunteers of Ireland moved to Rawdon's right front, a "Corps of Convalescents" to his left. Greene's apparent failure to foresee that Rawdon's reserves would permit this turning of the tables is one of the counts raised by those who say he was not a sound tactician, however excellent as a strategist. Nevertheless, the unexpected appearance of Greene's artillery had shaken the British, and matters seemed to be going well for the Revolutionaries despite Rawdon's adjustment of his line, until trouble developed in an unlikely quarter, among Greene's most tested troops, the First Maryland.

Just what happened has always been disputed. Perhaps two sections of the regiment moved ahead of the rest, and the regimental commander, Colonel John Gunby, caused uncertainty and wavering in the whole unit by calling them back rather than advancing to join them. Perhaps the trouble began when Captain William Beatty was killed and his right flank company fell back in confusion, causing the adjacent company to do likewise. (Taking a leaf from the rebels' book, Rawdon had instructed sharpshooters to aim for officers.) In any case, in the midst of an advance Colonel Gunby seems to have ordered a halt to straighten his line, and then he ordered a retreat for the same purpose. In the retirement he lost control of his regiment. At this unlucky moment Colonel Benjamin Ford of the Fifth Maryland was hit and carried from the field, whereupon his regiment also broke. The Fourth Virginia on the opposite flank then ran as well, and only the Fifth Virginia remained to hold some sort of line.

They withdrew from the field deliberately enough to permit the other regiments to reform. For a time the artillery seemed sure to be lost, as a detachment of forty-five Marylanders sacrificed itself to the last man in a vain effort to keep the New York Loyalist dragoons away from the guns. William Washington's cavalry, however, returned from a wild goose chase of attempted encirclement of Rawdon's force at the last possible moment to rescue the guns by hitching them to their horses.

So Rawdon had won a tactical success, but in its effects Hobkirk's Hill was almost another Guilford Court House. Rawdon's losses approximated Greene's, 258 to 266; the Americans could much more readily find replacements, while the British were caught in a vicious circle because the tenuousness of their hold on their outposts kept them from recruiting Loyalist troops. As the British General James Murray had remarked at the beginning of the war: ". . . if the business is to be decided by numbers, the enemy's plan should be to lose a battle with you every week, until you are reduced to nothing." It was after Hobkirk's Hill that Nathanael Greene wrote his famous line: "We fight, get beat, rise and fight again."

Rawdon followed up aggressively with a series of maneuvers designed to unite his own force with Watson's and to compel Greene to do battle again on a field where the British would hold the advantage. He achieved his first aim, but Greene was as skillful as ever in avoiding a fight when he did not want one. Perhaps on the Murray theory he should have obliged Rawdon; but he felt his own losses and the vexation of Hobkirk's Hill deeply enough that for the present he preferred cheaper triumphs—such as resuming the elimination of British posts, which his setback at Hobkirk's Hill could not prevent.

Rawdon knew that if necessary Greene could again accumulate an army as large as the one he had led at Guilford Court House. When the effort to force another battle before Greene was ready proved futile, Rawdon consequently decided he must hasten trying to evacuate the posts scattered throughout the state in order to bring their garrisons together for a new field army of his own. He decided to abandon Camden itself—so that Greene would attain the result for which he had come to Hobkirk's Hill after all— and to order the immediate abandonment of Ninety-Six and Fort Granby as well. Fort Granby, near the site of Columbia, was a link between Camden and Ninety-Six.

Meanwhile Marion and Lee were attacking Fort Motte, at the place where the Congaree and Wateree meet to form the Santee. Rawdon hoped to relieve this post on his

way from Camden to the sea. The Revolutionaries were
going about the deliberate business of constructing formal
siege approaches when Rawdon's campfires appeared in the
distance on the High Hills of Santee. Lee thereupon proposed to set the principal feature of the fort, the Motte
family house, afire with flaming arrows. The usual resident,
Mrs. Rebecca Brewton Motte, a rebel, was in the besiegers'
camp, and she readily assented, producing an East Indian
bow and a bundle of arrows to do the job. On May 12 the
arrows were fired, a cannon drove off men trying to put
out the flames, and despite Rawdon's approach the fort
surrendered. The fire being put out, Mrs. Motte had time
to entertain the officers of both sides at dinner.

Thomas Sumter had neglected to heed Greene's appeal
for reinforcement before Hobkirk's Hill because he was
occupied with his own plan to capture Fort Granby. The
effort turned into another of Sumter's now considerable
succession of fizzles, but undaunted as usual the Gamecock
went on to try his hand against Orangeburg, about fifty
miles south of Granby on the North Edisto River. Historians have disagreed whether the garrison here numbered
350 or only 85, but Sumter had over a thousand men, and
he invested the place and frightened it into surrender with
a few rounds of grapeshot on May 11, the day after Rawdon
left Camden. For several days thereafter Sumter's men
amused themselves by annoying Loyalists throughout the
neighboring countryside.

This activity prevented Sumter from having another
shot at Fort Granby, because Henry Lee and his Legion left
Fort Motte on May 13 for a fast march to Granby, arriving
on the 15th. A Loyalist garrison was still present, because
Rawdon's orders to evacuate had fallen into rebel hands.
Like Sumter before him, Lee found Fort Granby a strong
stockade; but he had heard that the commandant, Major

Andrew Maxwell of Maryland, was an uncommonly ava-
ricious individual, and this information gave him hope that
good things might follow a mere summons to surrender.
Having unlimbered a six-pounder and fired a couple of
shots over the stockade, Lee sent the infantry of his Legion
in a menacing march with fixed bayonets to a point just
beyond the fort's musket range. Then he delivered his summons. Major Maxwell behaved as anticipated by replying
that he was willing to yield the fort and its public stores
if he and his men could go to Charleston under parole and
keep their private property. His definition of private
property proved to include two wagonloads of plunder from
rebels' houses and farms. There occurred a brief quibble
over whether horses should be included in the surrender,
but Lee received word from Sumter that Rawdon was coming upcountry to attempt a rescue. Thereupon Lee gave
Maxwell the most generous interpretation of the terms, in-
furiating a party of Sumter's men who had reached the
scene, but gaining without a single loss a fort, two cannon,
the garrison's other weapons, an ammunition supply, salt,
and liquor.

When Sumter arrived, he was so exasperated over his
own failure to be the captor of this rich haul, and over his
troops' anger at Lee's generosity, that he sent a letter to
Greene announcing that he was resigning his commission.
The effective word here is "announcing"; he could not
actually resign to Greene, because the commission was from
South Carolina, Greene was a Continental officer, and Governor Rutledge was far away in Philadelphia. Greene took
advantage of this technicality to write Sumter a conciliatory
letter appealing for reconsideration, and to offer a series of
mollifying gestures. Whatever Sumter's faults, Greene did
not want to lose his inspirational presence. In the sequel he
persuaded Sumter to stay, but part of the price he paid

was an at least partial recognition of "Sumter's law" as a basis for enlisting troops. "Sumter's law" was Sumter's promise to recruits that he would pay them in plunder taken from Tories. Greene applied to this purpose the Negro slaves taken at Granby. Needless to say, Sumter's law helped brutalize the war still further.

Another post ripe for the plucking was the one at Georgetown, off the mouth of the Pee Dee. This place was almost Francis Marion's home, and taking it was a project especially dear to his heart, the more so because he had already tried twice and failed: in November, 1780, when his nephew had been murdered by Loyalists in the course of the attempt; and in January of the current year, when Lee and Marion together forced their way into the town and captured the British commandant, but without artillery or scaling ladders found themselves unable to take the fort. Marion's desire to gain Georgetown was strong enough to cause him to give Sumter a taste of his own medicine, when Sumter called on Marion to co-operate in his own latest schemes, while Marion hastened down the Pee Dee instead. Marion contended that although Sumter held a South Carolina commission as brigadier general antedating his own, he was now on Continental service responsible to Greene, and his commission as lieutenant colonel commandant of the Second South Carolina Regiment made him Sumter's superior in that service. More than that, he had heard that the Georgetown garrison was reduced to eighty British and Loyalist soldiers, and he was not to be denied the consequent opportunity. On May 28 he appeared before the fort and had his men begin building approaches. Rather than stay to surrender, the garrison took to boats and fell down to Charleston. With Georgetown his, Marion responded to orders from Greene to co-operate with Sumter after all, a role in which he was unfortunately unable to prevent new blunders by the Gamecock.

Henry Lee and his Legion, meanwhile, along with some newly raised North Carolina militia under Major Pinketham Eaton, moved on Greene's orders to join Andrew Pickens's South Carolina men and Colonel Elijah Clarke's Georgia troops in laying siege to Augusta, Georgia. Lee advanced swiftly, letting his infantry take turns riding his cavalry's horses, because Greene feared that the garrison of Ninety-Six would march to the relief of Augusta. Swiftness won an unanticipated dividend when Lee heard that the King's annual presents to the Indians of Georgia and the western Carolinas were deposited at Fort Galphin, or Fort Dreadnought, in South Carolina, the stockaded home of the deputy superintendent of Indian affairs some twelve miles from Augusta. Lee took the place easily by staging a weak mock attack which drew out the garrison for a sortie, whereupon Lee walked in with his main force to take a plentiful supply of ammunition, small arms, clothing, blankets, medical stores, and provisions.

Augusta was a tougher nut to crack, but Lee's reinforcement gave the besiegers something over 1,500 men against some 330 Loyalist militia and 300 Creek Indians. The rebels were able to storm an outlying work and capture its cannon to turn them against the main fort, and they built another Maham tower. By June 4 they thought they could carry the place by assault, and the garrison thought so too. The Revolutionaries issued the customary summons as a preliminary to the proposed assault, and the garrison accepted the summons, agreeing to surrender on condition they be marched under safe conduct to Savannah and paroled. It required a strong guard of Lee's Continentals to enforce the safe conduct against the Georgians and South Carolinians. Except for the coastal strongpoints of Charleston,

Savannah, and Wilmington, only Ninety-Six now remained as a garrison of the Crown in the Carolinas or Georgia; Rawdon's order to evacuate that place had miscarried like the order for Fort Granby.

While this inexorable, even monotonous, process of chopping off forts was taking place, Colonel Welbore Doyle and a party of New York Loyalist Volunteers found and destroyed Francis Marion's main base of operations, Snow's Island, among the swamps of the Pee Dee. This feat, which had eluded Banastre Tarleton in his heyday, now availed the British nothing; Greene and the rebels had too firmly grasped control of the momentum of the war. The only hope of reversing that momentum, Rawdon still thought, was to return to the field with a sizeable army to challenge Greene to battle. Little as fighting battles had profited Cornwallis at Guilford Court House or Rawdon himself at Hobkirk's Hill, to fight nevertheless seemed preferable to waiting and watching while the rebels reconquered the South. The miscarriage of Rawdon's order to evacuate Ninety-Six proved to present him with his opportunity.

Ninety-Six: May 22–July 1, 1781

"Weather incidentally is an important factor too often discounted in explaining events of eighteenth-century military operations."
—Eric Robson, *The American Revolution*

While Marion dealt with Georgetown and Lee and Pickens with Augusta, Greene himself marched on the last and toughest of the British forts in the interior of South Carolina, the post of Ninety-Six, seemingly so named because it was thought by its founders to be ninety-six miles from the

far frontier stockade at Prince George on the Keowee River.
Ninety-Six guarded the paths from the over-mountain country and the land of the Cherokee to both Charleston and
Savannah. Its garrison consisted of 550 of the best of the
Loyalist troops, including the Second Battalion of the Loyalists of New York, the Second Battalion of New Jersey
Volunteers, and 200 South Carolina Loyalist militia. Their
commanding officer was Lieutenant Colonel John Harris
Cruger of New York, a soldier worthy of comparison with
the best on either side who held responsibilities just below
the highest.

Cruger was too good a soldier for Greene to be able to
afford mistakes against him, and unfortunately for Greene,
the siege of Ninety-Six more than any other event of his
Southern campaigns revealed that his tactical judgment was
not so consistently excellent as his strategic grasp. These
matters could not have affected the unbroken succession of
rebel conquests, however, had not Rawdon been able to
alter the strategic situation.

A siege it had to be, for Ninety-Six was too strong a
fort too strongly garrisoned to permit of any other approach
by Greene's force. Greene had with him 487 Maryland and
Delaware Continentals, 431 Virginia Continentals, and 66
North Carolina militia. Arriving in front of the fort on May
22, he began badly, being misadvised by the usually reliable
Kosciuszko, and concentrated his principal efforts against
the strongest part of the defenses. The original stockade had
been elaborated upon by a British engineer officer, who had
seen to the construction of an outlying fort with two block-
houses west of the main settlement and across a small creek,
to protect the water supply, and to the erection of the strong
Star Redoubt on commanding ground east of the settlement. The water supply was the most vulnerable point, but
Greene commenced digging approaches to the Star Redoubt

instead. He compounded his error by beginning the labor too close to the enemy's walls, and to these mistakes he added that of insulting the enemy by failing to comply with the traditional formality of first calling upon the garrison to surrender. Cruger responded by building a tall gun platform inside the Star and mounting his three three-pounder cannon upon it. Covered by their fire, a sallying party drove Greene's diggers from their work, and a party of black laborers filled in the rebels' approaches.

Greene resumed digging at a more respectful distance, and his parallels crept gradually closer to the fort through late May and early June, to the accompaniment of frequent but futile Loyalist sallies. Meanwhile he also carried out the form of summoning a surrender, although he laced it with another insult—again ill advisedly—by sending the summons by his adjutant general rather than in his own name and by not addressing Cruger by name; the significance of these little matters lies in their reflection of the asperity of rebel-Loyalist relations. Greene also prepared a Maham tower, which overlooked Cruger's gun platform and permitted riflemen to silence the artillery pieces on it. Cruger removed his artillery from the platform and had to restrict himself to firing his cannon at night. He did, however, raise his parapets enough with sandbags to enable his own riflemen. to continue firing effectively. When Greene added to the Fort Watson expedient of the Maham tower the Fort Motte expedient of firing flaming missiles at the enemy's roofs, Cruger had all his roofs torn off. The Loyalists in turn suffered disappointment when they failed in an attempt to set the Maham tower afire with heated shot; they could not improvise hot enough furnaces.

Henry Lee arrived from Augusta on June 8 and began belated operations against the western fort which protected the water supply. To that point a great deal of time had been consumed without much profit, and the implications of this unfortunate fact began to appear on the 11th. That day news arrived that Lord Rawdon had his field army at last and with it was marching to Cruger's relief; for the first time since 1778, reinforcements from the home islands numerous enough to be worth counting had reached the British army in America, and a heavy detachment of them had come to Rawdon in Charleston.

With the siege now become urgent, Lee next day sent a sergeant and nine privates to the western fort under cover of a dark (but rainless) storm, to try to set the place afire. They failed with a loss of six killed, but nevertheless within the next few days Lee worked his way so close to the creek that the only way for the garrison to draw water from it was to send naked Negroes with buckets at night. The growing thirst of the garrison was a serious matter, because the heat of a South Carolina summer was now bearing down on all concerned. It was too bad for the Americans that nobody had done this sort of thing earlier.

Greene sent Andrew Pickens with his militia and William Washington with all the cavalry to join Sumter in an effort to head off or delay Rawdon's advance. Marion received orders to enter the same activity, which he did. Unfortunately, Sumter was in general command of this enterprise, and assuming for some reason that Rawdon would come by way of Fort Granby, he removed his forces thence and away from the British army's path.

Rawdon was bringing 2,000 disciplined soldiers, including many who had fought with him at Hobkirk's Hill and the flank companies—the elite light infantry and grenadiers—of three regiments just arrived in America, the Third, 19th, and 30th. On June 17 a messenger pretending to be a sightseeing countryman ambled into Greene's camp and then succeeded in galloping on into the fort, with news that

Rawdon's relief was only thirty miles away. The garrison sent off a *feu de joie*, and as much as they were suffering from siege, thirst, and heat, they would not surrender before Rawdon arrived, unless Greene contrived to carry their works.

Greene considered marching to fight Rawdon and then returning to finish the siege, but the British reinforcements had changed the whole strategic balance by putting him back into the situation he had occupied when he decided he could not fight Cornwallis at Guilford in February. He did not have enough reliable and experienced soldiers. He therefore hoped to finish off Ninety-Six and then to escape; accordingly he scheduled an assault for June 18, Lee and Kirkwood to attack the western fort, while Lieutenant Colonel Richard Campbell of the First Virginia with a detachment of Virginia and Maryland Continentals attacked the Star. Lee and Kirkwood succeeded, but whether they could hold on would depend upon Campbell. The latter's men were making good progress in pulling down the sand-bags of the Star when two sallying parties rushed out to assail them on both flanks. Hard fighting followed, but the lieutenants commanding the Revolutionary advance parties were killed, and their men then fell back. Greene's assault had failed, and he had to break off the siege to escape Rawdon's oncoming column.

On June 21 Rawdon rode into Ninety-Six, saluting Cruger and his patient garrison. His acquisition of a field army apparently had ended the dreary succession of British set-backs. But it remained to be seen whether Rawdon could use his army to better effect than Cornwallis in bringing the rebels to bay.

When Rawdon entered Ninety-Six, Greene had put the Saluda River between his troops and the fort and was pressing on towards the Enoree. His cavalry, the infantry

of Lee's Legion, and Kirkwood's company formed a rear
guard to do the work some of these same troops had done
under Otho Williams in the race to the Dan. Rawdon took
up the pursuit, and he did so with an energy to rival Cornwallis's; his van was within sight of the American rear before
they crossed the Enoree.

But Greene crossed nevertheless, and as he pressed
farther, across the Tyger River and the Broad toward Charlotte, Rawdon decided to give up the pursuit at the Enoree.
Many of Rawdon's men had no sooner completed the arduous
crossing of the Atlantic than they had been rushed into the
march from Charleston to Ninety-Six. All his men had en-
dured that two-hundred-mile march at a forced pace in in-
tense heat, wearing heavy woolen clothing, moving over dusty,
parched roads through a country now desolated by years of
war. The novelist Kenneth Roberts has his Loyalist hero
Oliver Wiswell say of the siege of Ninety-Six: "Clearest of
my memories of South Carolina is that of the wilting heat.
It was sticky, dead, breathless. It made leaves hang limply
on the dusty trees, and seemed to hold in indefinite suspen-
sion the red dust that rose from beneath our feet." When
Rawdon's three regiments of reinforcements had arrived at
Charleston with only sixty sick and five dead on the crossing
despite its hardships, Colonel Frederick Mackenzie among
them predicted that the heat of the season would leave not
a quarter of them fit for duty by the end of the campaign.

Rawdon pulled back from the Enoree to Ninety-Six,
where he ordered the evacuation of the fort. He gave Cruger
part of his force to escort the garrison and Loyalist refugees
by a protected southerly route towards the coast, while he
himself with 800 infantry and 60 cavalry proceeded towards
a junction with the rest of the reinforcements on the Congaree. Even in relatively leisurely retreat, he lost fifty men
dead of sunstroke. Another pursuit like the race to the Dan

would have ruined Rawdon's army even more surely than Cornwallis's winter march had ruined his.

On July 1, as soon as he learned that Rawdon had turned back, Greene also moved southward again. Now he must gather all the rebel forces in the South and hope for recruits as he had done after the race to the Dan; for the balance of forces again decreed that as at Guilford Court House in March he must sooner or later slake the British thirst for battle. He must ruin Rawdon's army as he had ruined Cornwallis's, or the British would have it within their power to reverse his recent destruction of their outposts.

Eutaw Springs: July 1–September 8, 1781

". . . we came to the conclusion that we could not secure success if we struck swiftly. In consequence, *we resolutely chose the other tactics: To strike surely and advance surely.* In taking this correct decision, *we strictly followed this fundamental principle of the conduct of a revolutionary war: Strike to win, strike only when success is certain; if it is not, then don't strike.*"

—Vo Nguyen Giap

Having so recently been so close to complete mastery of South Carolina, the Revolutionaries could scarcely fail to feel an impatience to come to grips with Rawdon's new army, to try to restore the strategic situation which had followed Guilford Court House. Greene himself shared such impatience, and he hoped that by moving promptly southward he might find an opportunity to strike the British forces while they were divided. But after restraining impatience so often before, he was not about to gamble all he had already accomplished on a premature battle now.

Greene followed Rawdon cautiously towards the coast.

Learning that more of the British reinforcements, under
Lieutenant Colonel Alexander Stewart, were on their way
upcountry to meet Rawdon, he sent Lee and Kirkwood to
interpose between Rawdon and Stewart and try to delay the
latter, so that Greene might attempt to meet Rawdon sepa-
rated from both Stewart and Cruger. Rawdon with superior
numbers, however, simply pushed Lee and Kirkwood before
him and joined Stewart at Orangeburg. Greene assembled the
bulk of the southern forces in front of Orangeburg on July
10, including Sumter's men, Marion's, and William Washington's, and he contemplated doing battle. His forces now
outnumbered Rawdon's; but the British position was strong,
Rawdon remained superior in experienced troops, and
Cruger was not far away. Also, Greene's men like Rawdon's
were near exhaustion from their marches in the heat; Kirkwood's detachment had covered 323 miles in twenty-two
days. Greene withheld his strike.

Deciding that the time for assured success had not yet
come and that he could afford nothing less, Greene pulled
his men away to rest in the cooler and healthier region of
the High Hills of Santee. Sumter, Marion, and Lee, however,
would remain active enough to try to deny the enemy a similar rest.

Though Rawdon was youthful, the heat and the hardships of campaigning had undermined his health, and on
July 20 he sailed for England. He left behind, unfortunately,
a reputation blackened by the blame South Carolinians
placed upon him for the hanging shortly afterward, on most
dubious charges of espionage and treason, of Colonel Isaac
Hayne of the South Carolina militia—a blame somewhat
unjustly attributed, since primary responsibility in the case
rested with the commandant of Charleston, Lieutenant
Colonel Nisbet Balfour. Ahead of Rawdon lay better things,
including successful military leadership as governor general

and commander in chief in India when he was in his sixties, under his later titles of Earl of Moira and First Marquess of Hastings.

During the hottest weeks of the summer, Sumter, Marion, and Lee ejected the British Ninth Regiment from Monck's Corner and fought an engagement at Quinby Plantation. Sumter and Marion also quarrelled again, and their bad feeling reached a climax when a British privateer raided Georgetown, in part to retaliate against the application of Sumter's law. At this juncture Governor Rutledge happened to return to the state from Philadelphia, and he decided Sumter's law must be repudiated. The effect was to precipitate Sumter's retirement, a genuine retirement this time, and an unhappy ending to a military career which had been erratic enough but which had rescued South Carolina's resistance at the moment of deepest defeat.

By August Greene was ready to resume the quest for battle on favorable terms. The health of his men had responded to the relative coolness of the High Hills, and perhaps more to the point, a new brigade of Continentals had arrived from North Carolina. He broke camp on August 22. Responding to his movements, Colonel Stewart, now leading the British field forces, took position near a brick plantation house and a palisaded garden at Eutaw Springs. There Greene decided to attack him.

To a degree, Greene was yielding to impatience after all. His numbers merely equalled Stewart's, and in general such odds were bad. Stewart commanded about 2,000 men, including Cruger's three Loyalist battalions from Ninety-Six; the flank companies of the Third, 19th, and 30th Regiments; the battalion companies—that is, the remaining portion—of the Third; the 63rd and 64th Regiments, both much reduced by campaigning; and a small South Carolina cavalry regiment. What emboldened Greene to move upon Stewart was

the unusually high quotient of experience in his own army.
He had over a thousand Continentals, including the proven
Maryland, Delaware, and Virginia troops; Lee's Legion and
Washington's cavalry; and almost 700 South Carolinians of
Sumter's, Marion's, and Pickens's forces, not masters of
parade-ground precision but thoroughly hardened by many
months of war. With such men, Greene believed he no longer
needed the heavy numerical advantage of Guilford Court
House.

Greene approached Stewart's camp on the morning of
September 8. Stewart was not yet expecting him, and his
advance interrupted the work of a British detachment that
had gone out to dig sweet potatoes. The Revolutionary van
collided with Stewart's Loyalist South Carolina cavalry, who
were put to flight. Greene then moved to the attack in two
principal lines, once again employing the tactic of putting
his militia in front, his Continentals in another line behind
them.

The militia on this occasion included 150 North Carolinians who were militia of the usual sort, plus the South
Carolina partisans. All acquitted themselves with honor in
a stand-up fight somewhat broken by woods and thickets.
Because Stewart drew up the bulk of his force in a single
line, the militia were contending against nearly twice their
numbers. Greene said their "conduct would have graced the
veterans of the great King of Prussia." When at length a
counterattack by the 64th Regiment and Cruger's Loyalists
caved in the North Carolinians, Greene sent up the North
Carolina Continentals, who, though they themselves were
recent recruits, promptly restored the line.

Stewart now threw in such reserves as he had kept, and
once again the battle began to favor him. But Greene's
veteran Continentals had yet to join the action; Greene was
saving them for the moment of crisis. As the North Carolina

Continentals began to give way, he judged that moment
had come. Otho Williams's Marylanders and Richard Campbell's Virginians fired a volley and then sprang forward for
a bayonet charge. The infantry of Lee's Legion swung into
Stewart's left flank. The British Third Regiment stoutly
contested the advance of the Marylanders, but those finest
troops of the Continental Line at last prevailed. Only the
British flank companies under Major John Marjoribanks
remained standing, about 300 men, shielded by a thicket of
blackjack on what had been the right of Stewart's position.
They cut down a full half of Washington's cavalry as the
horsemen rode across their fire in an effort to find an
opening in the thicket; Washington himself was bayoneted
and captured. But Kirkwood's Delawares finally drove them
back.

Drove them back, but did not disperse them. Marjoribanks kept his battalion in hand and took up a new position
with Eutaw Creek to his right and rear and the palisaded
garden on his left. As Greene's victorious army continued
moving forward, they found themselves among the provisions and stores of Stewart's camp, near enough to Charleston and the sea to be rich beyond anything most of the rebels
could remember seeing. Amidst rum and brandy and solid
food, Greene lost control of his army. Except for the infantry
of Lee's Legion, some of the Marylanders under John Eager
Howard, and Kirkwood's Delawares, the rebel infantry became a drunken, gluttonous mob. Lee's and Kirkwood's infantry were still struggling with a British detachment which
had fortified itself in the brick house. Lee's horsemen and
Wade Hampton's South Carolina cavalry were grappling
with the South Carolina Loyalist cavalry. At this juncture
Marjoribanks fired a devastating volley into Hampton's
flank and then advanced into the American mob. His battalion captured two six-pounders which had been battering

the house and turned them against the Revolutionaries, pushed back Howard's Marylanders while wounding Howard himself, and led Stewart's rallied army in a general counter-attack which drove Greene's men into retreat. In the final exchange of firing, Marjoribanks fell mortally wounded.

His stubborn courage had snatched away from Greene the tactical victory which had eluded the American com-mander so long. Once again, however, Greene had gone to battle only when he could hardly fail to win a strategic ad-vantage. He said that Eutaw Springs was the most obstinate battle he ever saw, and the high casualties on both sides confirm the judgment—522 losses reported by the Americans (a figure including only eight missing, and therefore prob-ably minimizing the number lost in the disorder of plunder-ing the enemy camp), 693 reported by the British. If the American losses hurt Greene badly, however, and if Greene's lack of numerical advantage gives some ground for ques-tioning his decision to fight, Eutaw Springs still did to Rawdon's and Stewart's new army what Guilford Court House had done to Cornwallis's; it ended the army's days as an effective field force in the Carolina interior.

Like Cornwallis and Rawdon before him, Stewart was operating in a countryside where everything outside the range of his guns belonged to the rebel partisans. After 693 casualties out of some 2,000 men, he could not remain in that countryside. He called on Colonel Paston Gould, re-cently arrived as the ranking British officer in the province, to send out troops from Charleston to succor him. They reached him before Greene could take position for another strike, and together the British forces fell back to Monck's Corner, where Gould took command. Greene's third major battle and third defeat had left the British in control of no part of South Carolina except the immediate vicinity of Charleston.

The Fire Gutters Out: September 8, 1781–December 14, 1782

"Violence takes much deeper root in irregular warfare than it does in regular warfare. In the latter it is counteracted by obedience to constituted authority, whereas the former makes a virtue of defying authority and violating rules. It becomes very difficult to rebuild authority, and a stable state, on a foundation undermined by such experience."

—B. H. Liddell Hart, *Strategy*

In the civil war between rebel and Loyalist, too many hatreds had accumulated for the British withdrawal to the Charleston neighborhood to bring instant peace to the interior. The troops which had been Sumter's and those of Marion, Pickens, and Lee still had to range over the countryside avenging Loyalist raids and hoping to subdue their perpetrators. In North Carolina, Loyalists had struck from the coast to Hillsborough and carried away the governor of the state while Greene was waging the Eutaw Springs campaign, and the exploit went far to offset the effect of Stewart's retreat upon the morale of Loyalists in both Carolinas. When late October brought news that Cornwallis had surrendered to George Washington in Virginia, there was no implication of immediate respite for South Carolina; British troops more numerous than Cornwallis's still held Charleston, Wilmington, and Savannah.

At this hour, furthermore, Greene's army seemed on the verge of extinction. After Eutaw Springs the army had crawled back to the High Hills of Santee, once again exhausted by a summer campaign. Ten days after the battle, Greene counted fewer than a thousand men fit for duty,

while he tried to nurse 350 American and 250 British
wounded and growing numbers of malaria victims. "Never,"
wrote Lee, "had we experienced so much sickness at any one
time as we did now." The Virginia Continentals were due
to be discharged in December. On October 21 the Maryland Continentals, unpaid for two years, unclothed, a mere
200 men surviving from seven regiments, at last despaired
to the brink of mutiny. Some left the camps to test the
reaction and resolution of their officers. When roll calls
were announced, they returned. But while the officers lec-
tured them for their loss of discipline, a South Carolina
soldier named Timothy Griffin stumbled drunk into their
parade and shouted: "Stand to it, boys! Damn my blood if
I would give an inch." The next afternoon Greene had his
whole command watch while Griffin was shot for encouraging mutiny and desertion, an example which for the time
being quieted the others.

Cornwallis's surrender at least produced assurances from
Washington that reinforcements would march to Greene,
and with this encouragement and the return of cooler
weather, Greene marched down towards Charleston again
on November 8 to try to confine the British within the city
and keep their provisioning parties out of the countryside.
Fortunately, the events in Virginia had disheartened the
British more than Greene could yet know. The American
general decided to begin the new campaign by trying to cut
off a British garrison of some 850 men at Dorchester, on the
Ashley River fifteen miles northwest of Charleston. When
he approached on December 9 with 200 Maryland and Virginia Continentals and 200 horsemen from Lee's, Washington's, and Sumter's commands, the mere discovery of
Greene's own presence and the consequent assumption that
his whole army was upon them led the British to flee.

The reinforcements promised by General Washington

moved south only after painful delays, but Greene could
look forward to receiving 2,000 Continentals from Pennsylvania, Maryland, and Delaware under Major General Arthur
St. Clair at the beginning of 1782. When St. Clair's column
approached Wilmington, the British evacuated that place.
Henry Lee and Lieutenant Colonel John Laurens then led
an expedition against the former Wilmington garrison in its
new camp on Johns Island near Charleston. The effort failed
because crossing to the island demanded too delicate a
coordination with the low tides. Nevertheless, with the
arrival of St. Clair, Greene was able to mount an increasingly
tight blockade around the landward side of the city. He
did so even while sending Anthony Wayne off with some of
the reinforcements for the reconquest of Georgia, a feat
which Wayne substantially accomplished by precipitating
the evacuation of Savannah on July 11.

Behind Greene's protective lines the South Carolina Assembly resumed its sessions. The British in their last southern
stronghold, however, still stubbornly sent expeditions inland to penetrate Greene's blockade and feed themselves,
and their stubbornness still nourished lingering hopes
among the Loyalists and forced the South Carolina partisans
and Lee's and Washington's commands to be "constantly
kept on the alert, never stationary." The approach of warm
weather again, with still no end in sight, also strained the
patience of Greene's unpaid, unclothed, and badly fed troops
from distant places, and another incipient mutiny turned
up in April, this time among the Pennsylvania troops who
had staged the great mutiny of the war at Morristown at
the beginning of 1781. Greene again speedily executed the
ringleader as a warning to the others.

There were sad losses, too, as the war seemed to refuse
to die out. Young Colonel John Laurens, son of Henry
Laurens and himself already a member of the South Carolina

Assembly before the British capture of Charleston, lost his
life at Combahee Ferry on August 27 when he was caught
in an ambush while trying to run down a British provisioning party. Some historians count another action at Johns
Island on November 4, where Captain William Wilmot of
the Maryland Continentals was killed, as the last action of
the Revolutionary War.

But Cornwallis's surrender had indeed disheartened the
British more than either Revolutionaries or Loyalists could
know; and though orders and men moved back and forth
across the Atlantic with excruciating slowness and all such
reactions therefore made themselves felt only after long
delays, on September 6, 1782, a British fleet at last arrived
to conduct the evacuation of Charleston. Even then, ensuring
passage to some 3,800 Loyalists and more than 5,000 slaves
helped delay departure until December 14. Nathanael
Greene at last entered the city, still accompanied by troops
barely able to cover their nakedness. With the British army
gone, the Loyalists could no longer make effective resistance;
those who had not fled by sea or beyond the mountains
finally sought to become as inconspicuous as possible, to
limit the cruelty of the victors' last reprisals.

It is perhaps most remarkable of all the events surrounding South Carolina's history during the Revolution
that the last reprisals amounted to very little. Though the
final campaigns had centered in the lowcountry, and partly
for that reason the farms of the upcountry emerged in relatively good condition when peace returned, the devastation
of war had ruined everything but the natural richness of the
soil on many of the lowcountry plantations. Twenty-five
thousand slaves, a quarter of the prewar labor force of South
Carolina, were carried away in the course of the war. Equip-
ment had been seized and ruined. Only by going deeply into
further indebtedness could planters secure the means to put

in a crop in 1783. Everywhere, upcountry perhaps even more
than lowcountry, the war had been fought with ferocity
symbolized and nourished by "Tarleton's quarter" and
"Sumter's law."

Yet the return to order was notably rapid and complete.
The riots in Charleston between native merchants and arti-
sans on the one hand and factors of British merchants on
the other in 1783 and 1784 were a conspicuous exception
but a limited one. As early as 1784 the assembly passed a
statute easing the disabilities and penalties upon Loyalists,
albeit the purpose was to enhance the possibility of a return
of slaves to Revolutionary owners.

Almost every other seat of partisan warfare in the modern
world has found the return to stability a difficult or even
impossible task. The endless upheavals and civil wars of
modern Spain date from the guerrilla resistance against
Napoleon. The resort of some Frenchmen to irregular war
against the Germans in 1870 led directly to the Paris Com-
mune and contributed to a tradition of disdain for law
that remains one of the plagues of modern France. Though
other sources of instability are obviously present in the
Arab world, the legacy of Lawrence's nurturing of guerrilla
war against the Turkish Empire remains all too much a
reality of the contemporary Middle East. Yet South Carolina,
though it seethed in the early 1780's with the irregular
campaigns of Sumter and Tarleton, Marion and Ferguson,
returned in the later 1780's and the years which followed
not to renewed violence, but to a stability and internal unity
almost unparalleled even among the relatively tranquil histories of the states of the American Union.

Why South Carolina thus escaped a harvest of the grapes
of wrath which almost invariably spring from irregular war
is an intriguing question. Histories of the state in the immediate post-Revolutionary period are not notably suggestive

of answers. But contrasted with other modern arenas of irregular war, South Carolina was surely a land conspicuously favored by fortune.

Still, South Carolina in the nineteenth century was almost too firmly united and too distrustful of internal divisions for her own good health. Her unity in the nineteenth century has always seemed to bear earmarks of a *tour de force;* there was always a suggestion of strain and artificiality about her extreme discouragement of the rivalries of political parties and her studied centralization of state government. Perhaps at least one source of the uncommon unity which South Carolina cultivated in the nineteenth century lay after all in the state's unique experience with irregular war, with how dangerous and devastating internal disunity can become. Perhaps South Carolina so intently fashioned a monolithic politics because she could not risk a return to horrors of fratricidal conflict beyond anything which other states had known. Perhaps the uniqueness of latter-day South Carolina bears an as yet unexplored relationship to the uniqueness of her experience in the War of American Independence.

BIBLIOGRAPHY

Alden, John R. *The South in the Revolution, 1763-1789.* Baton Rouge: Louisiana State University Press, 1957.

Bass, Robert D. *Gamecock: The Life and Campaigns of General Thomas Sumter.* New York: Holt, Rinehart and Winston, 1961.

——————. *The Green Dragoon: The Lives of Banastre Tarleton and Mary Robinson.* New York: Henry Holt, 1957.

——————. *Swamp Fox: The Life and Campaigns of General Francis Marion.* New York: Henry Holt, 1959.

Billias, George Athan, editor. *George Washington's Generals.* New York: Morrow, 1964.

——————, editor. *George Washington's Opponents: British Generals and Admirals in the American Revolution.* New York: Morrow, 1969.

Boatner, Mark Mayo, III. *Encyclopedia of the American Revolution.* New York: McKay, 1966.

Clinton, Henry. *The American Rebellion: Sir Henry Clinton's Narrative of His Campaigns, 1775-1782, with an Appendix of Original Documents.* Edited by William B. Willcox. New Haven: Yale University Press, 1954.

Draper, Lyman C. *King's Mountain and Its Heroes.* Cincinnati: Peter G. Thompson, 1881; Spartanburg: The Reprint Co., 1967.

Gerson, Noel B. *Light-Horse Harry: A Biography of Washington's Great Cavalryman, General Henry Lee.* Garden City: Doubleday, 1966.

75

Greene, George Washington. *The Life of Nathanael Greene.*
3 vols. New York: Hurd and Houghton, 1867-1871.

Gregorie, Anne King. *Thomas Sumter.* Columbia: R. L.
Bryan, 1931.

Higginbotham, Don. *Daniel Morgan: Revolutionary Rifle-
man.* Chapel Hill: University of North Carolina Press,
1961.

James, William Dobein. *A Sketch of the Life of Brig. Gen.
Francis Marion and a History of His Brigade.* Charles-
ton: Gould and Riley, 1821; Marietta, Ga.: Continental
Book Co., 1948.

Johnson, William. *Sketches of the Life and Correspondence
of Nathanael Greene.* 2 vols. Charleston: A. E. Miller,
1822.

Lee, Henry. *Memoirs of the War in the Southern Depart-
ment of the United States.* New York: University, 1869.

McCrady, Edward. *The History of South Carolina in the
Revolution, 1775-1780.* New York: Macmillan, 1901.

——————. *The History of South Carolina in the Revolution, 1780-1783.* New York: Macmillan, 1902.

Moultrie, William. *Memoirs of the American Revolution.* 2
vols. New York: D. Longworth, 1802.

Ramsay, David. *The History of the Revolution of South-
Carolina.* 2 vols. Trenton: Isaac Collins, 1785.

Tarleton, Banastre. *A History of the Campaigns of 1780 and
1781, in the Southern Provinces of North America.* Lon-
don: T. Cadell, 1787.

Thayer, Theodore G. *Nathanael Greene: Strategist of the
American Revolution.* New York: Twayne, 1960.

Uhlendorf, Bernard. *The Siege of Charleston. With an
Account of the Province of South Carolina: Diaries and
Letters of Hessian Officers from the Von Jungkenn
Papers in the William L. Clements Library.* Ann Arbor:
University of Michigan Press, 1938.

Ward, Christopher. *The War of the Revolution.* Edited by
    John R. Alden. 2 vols. New York: Macmillan, 1952.
Willcox, William B. *Portrait of a General, Sir Henry Clinton
    in the War of Independence.* New York: Alfred A.
    Knopf, 1964.

9 780872 491335

THE PARTISAN WAR
The South Carolina Campaign of 1780–1782
Tricentennial Booklet Number 2
by RUSSELL F. WEIGLEY

From reviews

"An exciting examination of a comparatively little known episode in the American Revolution. Weigley, an American military historian, boldly states his theme in the introduction: in this era when unconventional or guerrilla war commands such an interest, it is instructive to view the South Carolina campaign against the British troops as an example of guerrilla war. . . . Because of his skillful writing and brilliant analysis, Weigley has written a book for a wide audience. Quotations from Giap and Mao Tse-tung enliven his comparisons. Brief, with no footnotes, but a selective bibliography, highly original, Weigley's booklet is an excellent introduction to the military history of the American Revolution." —*Choice*

". . . a splendid addition to the Tricentennial Booklets series. . . . offers provocative opinions on the struggle that raged through the Carolina back country in the early 1780's. . . . Professor Weigley has broadened our outlook and challenged us to re-examine our conception of the Revolution in South Carolina."
—*South Carolina Historical Magazine*

ISBN 0-87249-133-1

THE UNIVERSITY OF SOUTH CAROLINA PRESS
COLUMBIA, SOUTH CAROLINA 29208
www.sc.edu/uscpress

THE HIDDEN LIFE OF FAILED RELATIONSHIPS

HOW TO

BE A

BAD

FRIEND

KATHERINE SLEADD